MW01229781

The Exemplary Department Chair:

*Small Leadership and Advice
From the Stone Age*

Robert Birnbaum

Printed by author   **ISBN:** 9798840968284   *August 2022*

Copyright

.

Acknowledgments

I want to thank Dr. David Lefevre, Chairman of Limited, and John Challice, Vice President and Publisher of Oxford University Press, for permitting the inclusion in this book of materials that I originally prepared for an online, interactive computer-based course of study called "Leadership and Management Approaches" published by Epigeum Limited, now a part of Oxford University Press.

My grandson, Robert Birnbaum, was instrumental in resolving all my computer issues. Newer generations can do things older generations can't.

The cover picture is courtesy of Shutterstock. It may appear to show the raised hands of people clamoring for attention, something that a Chair might encounter in Chapters One, Two, and Three. In reality, these are stone-age hand stencils created by our ancestors, fitting as an illustration for Chapters Four, Five, and Six.

Table of Contents

Introduction

This book is for academics who currently are department Chairs or are thinking about becoming one. I am going to look at the Chair's role from two perspectives. The first is based on reports by psychologists and sociologists who have analyzed small-group leadership. An academic department is a prototypical small group, and I suggest that Chairs can become more effective by adopting evidence-based recommendations about effective leadership in such settings.

The second perspective is based on the discoveries of anthropologists and archeologists who have considered how human leadership was enacted in groups 20,000 years ago. It incorporates some ideas about brains, genes, and memes and proposes how Chairs can become more effective by adopting some of the leadership practices of our Stone Age ancestors.

Suggestions about what Chairs can do to make themselves and their department more successful must be seen in the context of academic institutions' shared values and traditions. For this reason, I will emphasize the Chair's role in fulfilling colleges' social and educational purposes and the interests of those who work within them. Most importantly, I will explore why some Chairs become leaders while others do not and offer common-sense proposals that make leadership more likely. I hope this book will help Chairs and Chairs-in-Waiting to:

- Appreciate how you can influence your colleagues to improve their professional skills within the context of academic morality;
- Understand how different sources of power available to leaders affect what you can do and how you can do it;
- Apply some principles and techniques that should increase your effectiveness in an academic, professional environment;
- Learn how influence can be gained and lost and what you can do over time to maintain influence with your colleagues and within your institution;
- Gain insight into how and why your leadership can promote collegiality, trust, motivation, and accountability in your department;
- Consider the moral as well as the instrumental consequences of your behavior;
- Think about how leadership was enacted in the distant past and how your influence might be increased if you adapted some ancient practices and became a Stone-Age Chair;
- Think about why only a relatively small number of department Chairs become leaders and how you can become one of them.

Dilemmas of Leadership for Department Chairs.

Leadership advice is easy to find. There are books about leadership based on King David's biblical feats, the television exploits of the captain of the Starship Enterprise, and even the loveable stories of Winnie the Pooh, the Bear of Very Little Brain. Books have urged us, on the one hand, to follow the example of Jesus Christ, CEO, and on the other hand, to adopt the leadership principles of the Rogue Warrior. Books tout ten-minute guides, 22 vital traits, and 236 proven principles. There are books about the Eight Laws of Leadership, the Nine Natural Laws of Leadership, and the 21 Irrefutable Laws of Leadership. Perhaps this one-upmanship in the arms race of leadership laws has finally ended with the publication of *F*** Leadership* (Coats 2019). But I doubt it.

I'm not making any of this up! When I considered the plethora of research, writing, and sheer speculation about the topic, I felt thankful that we had not gotten to the point where there would be books titled *Leadership for Dummies* or *The Complete Idiot's Guide to Leadership.* A quick check at Amazon.com disabused me of that notion. To paraphrase what Sir Eric Ashby (1962:266) once said, the problem is that most books about leadership are no more convincing than books about how to make love.

If books on leadership in various settings don't seem helpful, you can read some valuable books on academic department Chairs' roles and activities. *Chairing an academic department* (Gmelch & Miskin 1995), *The department chair field manual* (Chu 2021), *The essential department chair* (Buller 2012), and *The academic chair's handbook* (Wheeler et al. 2008) all provide lists of Chair responsibilities and valuable hints on how to accomplish them. These books offer step-by-step suggestions about such essential topics as budgeting, faculty recruiting, and motivation. But they tend not to emphasize the personal and organizational factors that permit some Chairs, but not others, to become leaders.

College Management and Leadership

Management processes coordinate college activities and makes them function smoothly and efficiently. It is difficult, if not impossible, for leadership to exert influence in an organization without efficient management, and department Chairs are, among other things, managers. There is no secret to management. Most aspects are well understood, and I will suggest what Chairs can and should do to make their programs a little better - and their colleagues' lives a little easier. Management may seem to be about minor things, but the truth is that without managers, colleges can't run; without good managers, colleges become less efficient and effective. Fortunately, most academics who serve as Chairs can learn to be good managers. Some managers become leaders, and some do not, but most can make marginal improvements that, collectively, help their institutions become better places to teach and learn.

Although I must pay some attention to management, this book is primarily about leadership and how to influence others in specific ways. Influence in a group exists on a continuum ranging from predominantly coercive to predominantly non-coercive. Coercive influence usually involves one-way communication from a group member who applies force to others to ensure compliance even among the unwilling or the apathetic. I call one-way, coercive influence 'dominance' because it implies submission.

In contrast, non-coercive influence requires two-way communication between one group member and others, leading to their voluntary, active behavior as engaged participants. I define two-way non-coercive influence as 'leadership' because it implies willing followership. Leadership is not 'off 'or 'on,' but rather something that is 'more' or 'less.' Leadership involves mutually agreeable transactions among people whose social lives are based on their relationship with others (Fiske 1992:68). As we shall see, the mechanisms supporting the ideas of dominance and leadership have biological roots in the evolution of the human species, made possible by our genes and memes. I will have a lot to say about memes in Chapter Four.

Where We All Come From

We humans are newcomers. The Earth was created 4.5 billion years ago. Dinosaurs ruled the Earth 150 million years ago. The unknown animal that was the ancestor of both chimpanzees and humans lived 6 million years ago. But the first anatomically modern humans, *Homo sapiens*, evolved only 200,000 to 250,000 years ago in Africa. These early modern humans looked just like us. If you shaved one of our male ancestors, dressed him in sweatpants, a tee-shirt, and sneakers, and gave him an iPhone and earbuds, you wouldn't stare if you passed by him on Fifth Avenue in

New York City (this may not be a fair example, since New Yorkers are too blasé to stare at anything). All human beings alive today are related to those early people, so we can proudly say that we are all African in our roots.

Our species may have undergone a severe genetic bottleneck (a word used to describe sharp population reductions due to environmental events or human activities) about 70,000 years ago during the last Ice Age, leaving alive only between 1,000 and 20,000 humans (Jolly 1999; Boyd & Silk 2003; Dawkins 2004). Whether or not the "bottleneck" story is accurate, we are all descended from a small, common population. Humans are unusually genetically uniform (Boyd & Silk 2003), and our brains are universally similar. Not only are we all African, but we may all be kin. Too bad we don't act that way.

Natural selection shapes both our biological structures and our behavior. Looking at leadership from an evolutionary perspective permits us to consider several interesting new ideas. For example, humans' potential to lead and follow is instinctive and can be found in the hard-wiring of the human brain. This potential is a product of millions of years of evolution before and after our emergence as a species. Our ancient ancestors practiced a form of leadership we followed from about 50,000 years ago (or somewhat earlier) until 10,000 years ago, when humans first invented farming and animal husbandry. During this extended period, the meaning of leadership, long under primarily biological control, became increasingly influenced by language and other cultural elements.

Leaders today look at the complexities of globalization, technology, instant communications, and issues related to diversity in ideas, philosophies, people, and symbols. They may state with conviction that today's leadership is different and the problems more difficult, if not intractable, than ever before. Their claims might become somewhat more modest if they remembered that our ancient ancestors were confronted with extreme climate changes, fierce predators, aggressive or lethal neighbors, and no written history to guide their behavior. Their decisions meant life or death; today's decisions are often far less consequential.

'Small Leadership'

My suggestions in this book are based on behavior in small groups, both contemporary and ancient. Unless they become too large, college academic departments whose members know each other personally, see each other regularly, and meet together to engage in business at periodic intervals, are quintessential small groups. Leadership arises from interaction, so almost all authentic leadership takes place in small groups that permit leadership development based on relationships. As groups grow larger, interaction among members becomes increasingly challenging, groups become more hierarchically structured, and leadership (defined as non-coercive influence) becomes more problematic. Group size negatively affects effective group processes (Hollingshead et al. 2005).

Why is this so? As the number of members in a group increase, communications between them decrease. Interpersonal relationships are reduced, and it becomes more difficult for members to differentiate between the interests of other members and keep them in mind. The amount of time individuals can speak in meetings (to attempt to influence others) decreases, intimate contact between members becomes less likely, and groups are likely to fracture into subgroups. A small group of five people can have 75 possible pairs of relationships, and groups of 8 have 1,056 potential individual pairs of relationships (Tubbs 1978:105). Add in the other relationships created when members form differing subgroups, and the number of possible relations becomes enormous.

Some of the ideas in this book may apply to groups of any size, but I focus on what I call 'small leadership.' The human mind evolved when we lived in small groups in which we intimately knew how each person was related to everyone else. The outside (not the optimum) limit to 'small leadership' effectiveness in maintaining group stability is often considered to be no more than 150 people.

One hundred and fifty is called Dunbar's number after the primatologist who calculated it (Dunbar 2001). Dunbar studied how brain size affected the size of communities in which primates lived. The bigger the brain, the greater the number of animals that could live together to form a community. Dunbar determined that the smaller chimpanzee brain limited their viable group size to about 60-80 members. He then calculated that humans, with brains three times larger than chimpanzees, could form stable groups of up to 150 people. The problem is that to do so, they would have to spend 43 percent of their time talking and gossiping with each other.

A group that spends that much time gossiping has too little remaining for the other essentials of life (even in an academic department). And while 150 may be a reasonable limit for some groups, we shall see it is much too big for the kinds of internal and external interactions required by an intimate collegial unit.

I would set the group size in which 'small leadership' among humans can be practiced today at about 20, with a maximum of 40 under particular conditions. Everyone in a group of 20 or fewer can be a leader at some time and under some circumstances and a follower at others. It is not too difficult to practice 'small leadership' when people can overcome their natural tendency to dominate and control and focus instead on the equally natural human tendency to cooperate and share influence. Although this book focuses on department Chairs, many of my observations and suggestions would also apply to officials in charge of other comparatively small academic units. These could include deans of smaller colleges who meet regularly with their department Chairs and directors of administrative, service, or research groups who meet with their staff. Comparable small groups are also formed when a president regularly meets with her assistants and associate vice-presidents or a provost with his deans.

'Big leadership,' in academia involving much larger groups, bureaucratic structures, political systems, and different skill sets, is a topic for another book and another author.

Conventions

I have adopted certain writing practices for simplification and clarity. For example, I use 'college' to mean all two-year, four-year, and post-graduate non-profit, degree-granting institutions. All college personnel appointed to formal administrative positions are 'officials.' I assume that all department Chairs report to a 'dean,' and the highest official in the college is a 'president,' regardless of actual titles in specific situations. To highlight the book's audience and avoid losing sight of its purpose, I capitalize the word 'Chair' wherever it appears. I sometimes refer to the academic 'department' as a 'group' or a 'unit,' and 'institution' or 'organization' may sometimes be used instead of 'college.'

To the extent that I possess any areas of expertise, they are in leadership and academic organizations. I apologize to experts in fields outside these if I have not done justice to their ideas.

Benediction

A philosopher once said that "the ultimate business of education is human freedom" (Bailey 1976:76); by extension, I would say that the ultimate purpose of higher education is civilization. When you accept an academic management or leadership position, you are responding to that commandment. Why should you care? Because, as the poet John Masefield (1946:21-30) has said:

> There are few earthly things more splendid than a university... Wherever a university stands, it stands and shines; wherever it exists, the free minds of men, urged on to full and fair inquiry, may still bring wisdom into human affairs.

Department Chairs make the academic world go, and they also help define what the academic world is all about. I hope you find the materials in this book to be both stimulating and valuable as you work to make your institution 'stand and shine.'

Chapter One

Achieving Influence: A Primer for a New Chair

You probably didn't start your career in higher education with the explicit goal of becoming a department Chair. Almost no one does. Yet here you are – a successful scholar, teacher, practitioner, or researcher currently serving as manager and putative leader of just such a group or considering becoming one. You are likely an 'accidental official,' an academic charged with responsibilities for which you may not have been professionally prepared and for which most colleges offer little more than on-the-job training.

Colleges are often neither intentional nor coherent in preparing department Chairs. Two-thirds of all Chairs are given no formal training after their appointment, and of the one-third who do receive training, over 70 percent said it was for less than ten hours and didn't adequately prepare them for the job (Flarherty 2016). Most Chairs say they felt competent after six to 18 months. Whether this feeling of competence was related to their managerial tasks or leadership responsibilities is factually unknown, but I would guess it was the former rather than the latter.

So if you feel somewhat confused, you are not alone; many people in your situation initially do not feel ready for their jobs. You are likely to wonder: What do I do, and how do I do it? And your responses are important. Academic departments are the core of your institution.

They are the first-line units through which colleges fulfill their missions, serve students and the community, and directly engage in disseminating and discovering knowledge. Departments do the college's 'work .' The principal purpose of much of the rest of the college is to support them. Department Chairs probably have more significant impacts on the daily life of a college than any other officials.

Successful department Chairs come in both sexes, with different temperaments, shapes, sizes, colors, and various physical disabilities or limitations. Don't let stereotypes dissuade you from considering serving as a college official or lead you to prematurely predict the possibility of your success or failure as a potential Chair. At the same time, be realistic. You must recognize that those who will ultimately determine who the Chair will be are looking for achievements they expect to see in your earlier academic life. These will likely include advanced degrees, successful previous academic experiences in similar colleges, and (yes, it's true) even the status ranking of the colleges in your background (Birnbaum 1971). Regardless of your achievements, don't expect your successful experience as a Chair at Big City Community College will give you a leg up on being considered for a Chair position at Ivy Research University. And your professorship at Open Admission Public College may not carry much weight in your application to chair a department at Prestigious Private College. You may not consider such assessments 'fair', but making such distinctions are part of academic culture.

Is it Worth it? The Costs and Benefits of Being Chair

Serving as a department Chair has both advantages and disadvantages. The role may initially appear desirable - perhaps even glamorous - but it requires a level of attention to detail and responsiveness to the demands of higher-level officials many academics find unattractive. Is serving as a Chair worth it to you? Deciding whether or not to serve may be difficult. Some academics may agree to be Chair without fully considering how they may react to their responsibilities. Weighing the pros and cons may provide one way of reflecting on the match between your personal interests and the position's demands.

First, the good stuff. Being a department Chair may confer many professional and personal benefits. Professionally, it may enable you to improve the department's effectiveness by helping faculty members resolve problems, minimize bureaucratic hassles, and facilitate their teaching and research. It may allow you to engage personally with senior officials, get an insider view of college operations, and access institutional contacts and information.

Personally, it can beef up your resume, improve your chances for movement to other academic positions at your college, and enhance opportunities should you seek academic work elsewhere. It can give you a well-deserved sense of college and professional recognition and be a source of creativity and excitement. It may provide you with a profound feeling of having made a difference. And, of course, Chairs often receive increased compensation and perquisites not enjoyed by other department members. Perhaps there will be a reduced teaching load and a corner office (with a window!) in your future? Some studies have shown that 80 percent of Chairs are satisfied with their positions (Council of Independent Colleges 2016). What's not to like about being a department Chair?

Well, you should be aware that there may be some snakes in a Chair's Garden of Eden; here's what to watch out for. Even though deans and others may hold you accountable for problems created by department faculty, you are not their 'boss.' You may have some ability to influence your colleagues, but you will usually have little legal authority over them, and you usually cannot tell them what to do. Little authority – but lots of obligations.

The paperwork, constant meetings, and recordkeeping responsibilities of your new position may mean that you will have less time for teaching and research – the reasons you became a professor in the first place. Consequently, you may feel increasingly disconnected from academic life and advances in your discipline. Your days now may include more extended hours and increased stress. Constant interruptions and demands from higher-level officials, coupled with the 24/7 availability of email, may make it difficult to plan your day or separate your home and work life. These are some of the reasons that the department Chair has been called "the faculty job (almost) no one wants" (Zahneis 2022). Of course, you may be one of the "almost."

You may like your department colleagues (and you should never become Chair of a department whose members you don't like). Still, you may become frustrated by their apparent ignorance of general departmental and college policies and indifference to the fiscal constraints central to your everyday life. Some department members may blame you for activities or outcomes beyond your control; some may come to actively dislike you. Although most Chairs may be satisfied in their positions, only 25 percent plan on serving more than one term (Chu and Veregge. undated). You should think carefully about why this is so.

Which way does the scale tip for you? That is a question only you can answer. If it tilts towards the benefit side, and you think you can accept the negative aspects of the position with equanimity and good humor, you might find serving as a Chair a rewarding experience. If so, Great! But if it tilts towards the cost side, and you think you might continually be irritated by the inescapable realities of officialdom, management responsibilities might not be a good match for your interests and expectations.

And a mismatch is possible regardless of your professional stature or competence. Some of the unhappiest people in the academic world are great teachers or practitioners who agreed to serve as Chairs and regret later the changes in their professional responsibilities. And some of the happiest people are Chairs who relish their new roles and get pleasure from helping their colleagues remain productive and excited about their work. Consider being appointed with your eyes open. To test the waters at your college (the waters might be decidedly smoother or choppier at a different college), you might select three present or past department Chairs and informally interview them. Ask them what they found the most positive and negative aspects of the job, what they thought they had accomplished, and whether they would accept an appointment as a Chair in the future. Use their comments as a reality check of your views as you consider the pros and cons.

What is Your Objective?

A fundamental question if you are considering becoming a department Chair is - why? What is it that you want to achieve? If your primary motivation is to keep your program running smoothly as it responds to institutional requirements, you may be successful as a manager but not as a leader. Being a good manager is a reasonable ambition, but it may limit your ability to influence your department. Implementing new policies or programs will be challenging if you are only a manager. The greater the managerial effort and legal authority you use to effect change, the less likely you will succeed. On the other hand, success is much more likely when you also have the professional and moral authority provided by the department's willingness to accept you as a leader. You will be working with, rather than fighting against, your colleagues, and you may be successful in implementing improvements.

If you believe that your department can be made more effective and that you can influence group members voluntarily to move towards that objective, then perhaps you have the potential to be a leader. The possibility for leadership increases if your goal is consistent with the department members' manifest or latent values, even if they are not consciously aware of them. Purposefully creating new departmental values is difficult, if not impossible, but you can continuously remind your followers of values they have previously endorsed but may not have recently enacted. Your comments as Chair can be an effective way of getting department members to recall why they joined academia in the first place.

Even the best departmental members can find their ideals challenged by the constant need to attend to the daily problems of college life. As Senator Robert Kennedy is reported to have said, when you're up to your ass in alligators, it is difficult to remember that your original goal was to drain the swamp. If you wish to be seen as a leader by your colleagues, you as Chair must hold the alligators at bay so your department can do adaptive work.

Whether you are currently a department Chair or considering becoming one, it is essential to have some specific goal you believe the group can achieve if you wish to influence them as a leader. Leaders always ask themselves, 'what should be my goals, and how should I move towards them'? The goals need not be expressly or immediately articulated to the group (although it is important not to do anything contrary to them). Instead, you can hold them, as they say in the Vatican, *"in pectore"* until your acceptance by the department is complete and a propitious occasion presents itself. A goal need not be isolated, but only one of many you would like the group to achieve. And finally, although you may be influential in moving the group towards this goal, you can be considered a leader only if the group eventually endorses this goal voluntarily and without coercion.

What might such a goal be? Revise the curriculum; initiate post-tenure reviews; involve students in department decision-making; develop new teaching technologies; increase diversity among both faculty and students; become more teaching-intensive; reduce student attrition; bring peace to a contentious department; initiate a new program; collaborate with other departments inside and outside of your college; become more research-intensive; build community service into your curriculum; develop a distant learning program and provide necessary faculty training to implement it. Don't like any of these? That's O.K. Select an idea of your own. But whatever you decide, you should not initiate new ventures until you have been Chair long enough to know what your followers want, fully understand the department's strengths and weaknesses, and have a good sense of what you could do to improve it. Whatever you choose, your goals should be consistent with the interests and capabilities of your department colleagues. At least once a year, you should work with unit members to assess formally the extent to which your unit has moved towards the goal(s) you are reaching for, what mid-course corrections you have to make, and what your next steps might be.

Within a week of taking over the Chair, you will likely find dozens of things you could do to improve your department. Control your impulse to take immediate action. Almost every existing policy, program, or procedure exists because someone wanted it. You had better become a knowledgeable student of department history before you step on someone's pet scheme.

So You Are a Person of Influence. Now What?

Let's assume that you have considered your goals and decided to accept the Chair. Now what? Becoming a Chair makes you a Person of Influence in your department and confers specific responsibilities and obligations. You will have to transition from a content expert to a manager and, perhaps, a leader. This is true in any organization, but it is particularly salient in universities because academics frequently move between faculty and department Chair roles. Depending on your relationships, you may find a former Chair, now a faculty member in your group, who can either be a sound advisor or a perpetual second-guesser and irritant.

If you are a former faculty member, you may have previously negotiated a role in your college. But when you become a Chair, you may have to alter many of your behaviors and relationships because your view of the department and the college will change. You will develop new habits of mind, and department members may revise how they interact with you (and you with them). Your colleagues often understand and accept your interest in moving from primarily teaching to administering. Still, some may see it differently – potentially (at the extreme!) as a rejection of professional values or as moving from 'one of us' to 'one of them.' Some faculty members may wonder why a respected scholar would give up the pleasures of teaching and research to become an official. They may question whether you can be trusted in your new role. Half-jokingly and half-seriously, they may express condolences to you when your appointment is announced. If you come from outside the college, they may greet you warmly yet warily and then watch suspiciously to see if you have the right stuff. Your initial behavior may be critical. First impressions may color how your colleagues view you and may be difficult to change.

Department members and department Chairs do different things and meet different people. Because they are exposed to different environments, they come to have different perspectives. Conflicts are expected between officials and the groups they supervise, but disputes can take different directions. They can be personally disagreeable but at the same time a valuable source of innovation and change.

Department members usually recognize and appreciate that Chairs have different roles and expectations. They are often willing to overlook some strange behaviors as long as they believe you understand what faculty members do and respect them as fellow professionals. They are more likely to accept you if they see that you effectively represent their interests when discussing the department and its needs with the dean and other senior officials.

Fulfilling these expectations may prove to be trickier than it sounds. As an official, you will almost always find yourself 'in the middle' in at least three distinctive ways: between the interests of members of the department you serve and the dean to whom you report; between your dual roles within the department as both a colleague and as a supervisor; and between the conflicting desires to pursue your research and intellectual life while you also attend to your demanding official responsibilities. Being 'in the middle' means you may have to respond continuously to somewhat different, often incompatible, expectations of your behavior and activities.

The dean and the college expect you to ensure that the department you are responsible for functions efficiently and effectively. They will see if you are responsive to the interests and needs of those above you in the organizational hierarchy, even if your department members do not support some of these organizational interests or needs. Simultaneously, department members expect you to serve their interests and needs, even if they occasionally conflict with college policies. The supervisor/colleague dichotomy works the same way. As a supervisor, you will be expected to prioritize the college's hierarchical, structural, and control needs to comply with policies and procedures. But as a colleague, you may be under pressure to give precedence to the group's needs for autonomy and self-direction, which may mean sometimes protecting it from the very college policies you are committed to upholding. A Chair must reconcile these differences so that group members contribute to the department and the college's mission while meeting their personal growth and self-expression needs. In addition to these difficulties, potential department Chairs must accept the possibility of failure. Your ability to manage these tensions will prove critical to your success. A Chair has to have both academic and managerial smarts to be effective

The Three Paths of the Chair

I believe that Chairs follow one of three paths that can lead to either being an Average Chair (the most common type), a Failed Chair (often the consequence of a poor match or a hostile environment), or an Exemplary Chair (which is what we would all like to be). I estimate that about half of all Chairs are Average, and a quarter are Failed or Exemplary. The following descriptions of the three paths of the Chair are taken from analyses of other campus leaders (Birnbaum 1992).

Average Chairs appreciate and value their new status and are willing to accept the inconveniences of the role in exchange for the opportunities it may provide. They work hard, do what the dean requires, and are generally supported by their department members. Their departments may not change markedly for the better during their service, but at the same time, they are unlikely to deteriorate either.

Failed Chairs may initially have been intrigued by their new role but then discover a misfit between what the position requires and what they are either able or want to give. Due to lack of patience, unwillingness to listen to or consult with department members, or disinterest in management activities, the Chair gradually loses the support of both the dean and department members (although the Chair may be too insensitive to realize this). Whether the Chair remains in office due to inertia or leaves (either voluntarily or not), the group's performance and morale are likely to suffer.

Exemplary Chairs directly confront the problems inherent in their position and find satisfaction in the opportunities the role offers to help the department and the college improve. They maintain their enthusiasm, institutional commitment, and desire to interact constructively with department members throughout their appointment and are seen by others as combining competence with sensitivity to social dynamics. They want certain things for their department and work to get them. Their departments are likely to have improved as a consequence of their service. Exemplary Chairs are admired by their group members and considered by their dean to be a significant college asset. Later we will discuss what Exemplary Chairs can do and why they can do them.

Charisma

Both managers and leaders are likely to have some degree of charisma, although of different kinds. 'Charisma' was defined by Weber (1947: 358) as

> *a certain quality of an individual personality by virtue of which he is set apart from ordinary men and treated as endowed with supernatural, superhuman, or at least specifically exceptional powers or qualities. These are such as are not accessible to the ordinary person, but are regarded as of divine origin or as exemplary, and on the basis of them the individual concerned is treated as a leader.*

This definition of 'charisma of person' originated in a religious context and depicted an almost god-like figure. Charisma was used to describe the conspicuous personal aura around great and unusual people such as Mother Teresa, Winston Churchill, Martin Luther King Jr., and John F. Kennedy. Today, it usually refers to the personal magnetism and persuasiveness that seems to radiate from some people and inspires devotion in others. Personal charisma also requires likeability. While we typically think of personal charisma as a positive trait, remember that evil people, such as Hitler, have also been considered charismatic. Many con men have personal charisma, which is why they are so good at separating us from our money.

If leaders can increase their influence with the charisma of person, managers increase their influence through the charisma of their office. 'Charisma of office' routinizes charisma through hierarchical, bureaucratic structures and titles and provides a means in the modern world by which even people who are not particularly likable or competent can exert influence. Acquiring titles such as president, dean, or department Chair may not induce the 'awe' suggested by the original concept of charisma. Still, titles evoke respect and esteem, particularly from those who occupy lesser roles. We bow to the Queen of England and don't speak to her unless first spoken to. We rise for the President of the United States. The Pope is never formally introduced because he needs no introduction.

The primary differences between management and leadership are due to the sources of their authority and how department members respond to them. As a manager, you will have charisma of office. Your influence will come from the legal authority granted to you from above, not necessarily from your personality or how your colleagues view you. Your superiors and department members have a right to expect you to be well-organized, efficient, able to utilize available resources, and responsive to the requests of their administrative hierarchy for data, information, and decisions.

Will you also be a leader? That depends. Leaders influence others by inspiring their trust and motivating them with words and deeds. Unlike your charisma of office, your influence as a leader is not based on specific legal authority from above but on the professional and moral authority ascribed to you by your department. Your right to a leader's influence can only be conferred voluntarily from below by your department colleagues in response to your personal charisma.

Chairs thus have two potential sources of authority. As a manager, you always have legal authority granted from above; as a potential leader, you may also have professional and moral authority vested from below. The most effective formal leaders have charisma both of person and office, enabling them to exert influence over and above ordinary officials.

What Your Department Wants From You

Most of your department members joined the academic profession because there were limited opportunities to work in their chosen discipline and develop a fulfilling life without a college appointment. Maybe they were motivated to associate themselves with your particular college because its values were consistent with theirs; perhaps they chose it as a convenience. In either case, they believed the institution would provide an opportunity for them to exercise their expertise and further develop mastery in their field.

Once on the faculty, their relationship with your department is even more critical than their identification with the college. This emphasis on the department rather than the institution is not surprising since departments likely consist of colleagues with similar interests and methodological training. Departments provide members with opportunities for collegiality and interpersonal interaction. They are also the locus for allocating resources academics care about, such as office space, laboratory facilities, clerical support, and teaching assignments. This emphasis on the department, instead of the college, increases the consequences of your behavior as a Chair. As declining resources make it increasingly difficult for the college to offer tangible rewards, the department remains the primary source of the intangible and symbolic benefits of great value to faculty members.

To provide service to your department, you must understand what members desire and what they find distasteful. While different departments have different interests, academics generally have been self-selected and pre-socialized to agree on some fundamental values and behaviors. These common predispositions will affect how department members assess you and facilitate or limit what you might achieve. Your department will be more likely to accept your influence if they believe that you share their academic values, and they will be less likely to think of you as 'one of us' if you don't. Good managers are expected to provide some of these at least sometimes. Good leaders are expected to demonstrate most of them most of the time. So what do they want?

Academic freedom. The right to teach in their area of expertise, do research of their choosing, and engage in other professional activities without unreasonable restrictions or fear of reprisal.

Autonomy. The right to behave according to their professional judgment, without the need for supervision or the approval of others.

Collegiality. The right to belong to a cooperative and respectful group of peers, functioning in a climate of openness, trust, and courtesy, in the common pursuit of collective objectives.

Participation. The right to have their voice heard and be involved in making appropriate decisions, either personally within the unit or through representatives at the institutional level.

Support. The right to be provided with the necessary and proper facilities, materials, supplies, and ancillary personnel needed to perform their professional responsibilities.

Recognition. The right to have their contributions understood and appreciated within the department and college and to have their achievements acknowledged within the professional community.

Environments, shared perceptions and values, commitments to collegiality, participation in governance, and the availability of support resources may all be affected by institutional culture and history over which you may have no control. You may not always be able to provide members of your department with some of the rights they expect. Nevertheless, you can facilitate their professional work if they know that you share their concerns, have their backs, and are committed to improving department and college conditions to the extent you can.

Conspicuous by its absence on the list of things that group members want is 'money.' Your colleagues are not indifferent to financial considerations. Still, they entered academic life knowing that higher education was not the road to riches. They joined your department because of their passionate commitment to a specific discipline; they are likely to consider what they do more a 'calling' than a job and believe that serving faculty and students in a college gives their lives a particular and larger purpose. For them, the coin of the realm is not money but autonomy, recognition, and prestige.

What Your Department Doesn't Want From You

Your department is likely to be relatively content with you as their Chair if they see that you recognize the desirable rights mentioned above to the extent you can. However, even when these institutional conditions are present, you can undermine your ability to exert influence if you engage in behaviors that members of your department are likely to find offensive. They may dislike you, but academic groups will almost certainly continue to do their jobs even as they reluctantly comply with your legal directives. However, you will likely find it impossible to exert any other influence on them. Behaviors that you and any other official must avoid include:

Disrespect. Department members are likely to reject your influence if you are not seen as identifying with and respecting the department, individual department members, or the disciplines or professional activities in which department members engage.

Officiousness. Department members are likely to reject your influence if they believe that you continually invoke the rights inherent in your appointment as an official, abuse your authority by improperly allocating rewards and punishments, make unilateral decisions without providing reasons to department members, undermine department member prerogatives, give precedence to self-interest as opposed to department interests, or act in the department's name without prior consultation.

Entitlement. Department members are likely to reject your influence if you are seen to solicit and/or accept special treatment for yourself, give privileges or preferential treatment to some group members but not others, or evaluate individual colleagues using personal criteria and standards unrelated to their professional activities.

Irresponsibility. Department members are likely to reject your influence if you violate institutional regulations, consistently fail to prepare and submit requested data and reports in an accurate and timely manner to the college hierarchy, do not manage group resources effectively, mishandle institutional funds, bend to pressure, o2r blame others for your own failings.

Disengagement. Department members are likely to reject your influence if you publicly disparage your department or college or fail to defend the department if its quality, performance, or commitment are questioned.

Impropriety. Department members are likely to reject your influence if you engage in behavior that brings disrepute to the department, cannot work collaboratively with other officials, alienate others in the college hierarchy, or engage in improper conduct with students.

The Luminous Chair

Becoming a Chair requires you to transition from being an expert in a specialized field to being an official with specific responsibilities. Renegotiating your college role exposes you to the conflicts inherent in 'being in the middle' between your department members and the college hierarchy, and within a department that sees you simultaneously as both colleague and supervisor. These inherent contradictions will put you in a position of 'liminosity' (Freeman, Karkouti, & Ward 2020), which anthropologists use to describe a life stage of ambiguous transition between what you have been and what you are to become. Managing these tensions will prove more important than your personal or physical characteristics. Supporting what department members want, and avoiding behaviors they dislike, will go a long way to establishing your successful term as Chair.

Chapter Two

Academic Management

Management may be extremely important even though managers are indistinguishable. It's hard to tell the difference between two different light bulbs also: but if you take all light bulbs away, it is difficult to read in the dark (March 1984:27)

Many scholars and practitioners have attempted to differentiate the concepts of 'management' and 'leadership,' and their definitions (particularly of 'leadership') vary. This is how I distinguish the two terms. Management is an organization function designed to improve efficiency, performed by appointed officials. Leadership is the ability to influence others by inspiring trust and motivating them through words and deeds. As we shall see, these generalities hide a myriad of subtleties. Whether behavior looks like that of a manager or a leader may be affected by the specific situation. This is particularly true in organizations, such as colleges, that have 'process cultures' where what you do and how you do it are equally important. People in colleges are as concerned that the processes were conducted in ways they consider legitimate as they are with the outcomes of the processes

The unusual governance processes of colleges often blur the lines that supposedly differentiate between management and leadership. It is sometimes difficult to tell the difference between them because managers and leaders often do the same things and have many of the same characteristics. For example, managers and leaders are equally likely to be intelligent, articulate, and able to synthesize information and persuade others. Their ability to persuade, and to be persuadable, stems in part from human nature. People are likely influenced by those in the group who have been successful (such as Chairs) and copy their language, dress, and behaviors.

Your management effect as a department Chair depends on a tacit agreement in our society that your appointment as an official gives you the right to engage in certain activities and make specific requests. Members of your department, in turn, are obliged to comply. Our acceptance of the legitimacy of these mutual obligations is the basis for the effective functioning of colleges and other large and complex organizations. The legitimacy holds as long as you operate within the commonly accepted boundaries of the role, but not if you attempt to work outside it. Members of your department need not necessarily agree with your requests or decisions (although it would be helpful if they did); instead, successful management requires only that they acquiesce.

Chairs perform vital management tasks that support the department's work, help integrate it into college systems and support their goals. That means all Chairs must be managers. Some Chairs may also become leaders through processes that we will discuss later. For now, we will focus on mentioning some of the Chair's management tasks, which, if done well, can make everyone's life a little easier (and conversely, if done poorly, can create a toxic environment).

Academic Management Tasks

Although effective management is a critical component of institutional effectiveness, it is not highly valued in many colleges because it is often incorrectly seen as antithetical to academic values. The truth is that without managers, colleges don't run. Without *good* managers, institutions are likely to be neither efficient nor effective.

Some of your managerial tasks will be codified in institutional regulations; others will be idiosyncratic and may depend on individual interests, department history, and the current concerns of your dean. You can see the broad scope of your role in a partial listing of management responsibilities.

Personnel. Faculty development; orienting new personnel; monitoring individual performance; recommending salary and compensation; faculty recruiting; performance counseling; mentoring; supervising support staff; fostering diversity; assuring fair distribution of faculty work.

Academic program. New curriculum development; preparing the department strategic plan; preparing teaching schedules; chairing department meetings; negotiating with department members; managing program assessment; managing specialized facilities; student admissions, counseling, and marketing; coordinating with other departments/colleges.

Administration. Preparing department budgets; allocating equipment and travel funds; assigning office space; preparing and submitting all regular and ad-hoc reports; ordering and maintaining equipment; updating and maintaining records; interpreting college regulations; establishing internal communications systems; making sure that decisions get made and implemented.

Representation and Advocacy of the Department. Communications with senior managers, college administrative services, other institutions, alumni groups, external professional and academic groups, and funding and other support agencies.

Flak-catcher. Investigating allegations and complaints about department members; investigating allegations and complaints of students; resolving internal department disputes and conflicts; keeping problems off the dean's desk; responding to whatever comes along.

New challenges may be developing as well. Chairs will have to play a role in rethinking and restructuring higher education due to the Covid-19 pandemic and its aftermath (Gigliotti 2021). The development and maintenance of computer-based and other distance-learning processes, and the possibility of a continued need for social distancing in on-campus classroom settings, may place additional and unprecedented responsibilities on you. Revenues and department budgets may decrease for some time: massive layoffs or furloughs may become common, salary cuts may occur, instructional formats may have to be adjusted on the fly, and you may have to search for new faculty with non-traditional skill sets. You might have to increase your management activities' scope, likely decreasing faculty satisfaction. You may have to become a 'virtual manager' in which your contact with colleagues is restricted, meetings take place on computers, and the future changes daily.

Your management role as Chair is a classic case of having great responsibility but only limited authority. You may be asked to correct organizational or personnel problems (not of your making) that had not been attended to for years, improve a department's shaky quality and status, or transform a previously contentious group into a smooth-running and problem-free department. These outcomes may be unachievable under any circumstances but are likely incredibly complicated for Chairs, who usually have little discretion to make final decisions or additional funds to pursue such objectives.

You will also be responsible for relieving department members from spending their time writing reports, filling out forms, or doing other nonproductive or onerous tasks. Students of organizations refer to this role as 'protecting the technical core,' helping group members avoid taking time and effort away from their fundamental responsibilities. You may think of this as hassle management. Sometimes you can persuade upper-level managers to refrain from making such requests; you can often fail and end up doing them yourself.

An influential scholar of management (Mintzberg 1973) analyzed the activities of organizational managers. He described their role as requiring a lot of work, conducted at an unrelenting pace, and leaving little free time. Managers' activities were characterized by brevity, variety, and fragmentation and emphasized meetings. Managers preferred learning new organizational information that was current, specific, non-routine, and delivered verbally rather than in writing. Although this study did not include colleges, you will recognize that much of his analysis accurately describes your daily experiences.

A Chair's many and varied responsibilities can create real problems for you. It is often difficult to decide whether a specific problem reflects a significant issue or is instead trivia of the "you say po-tay-to, I say po-tah-to" variety. Urgent matters identified by department members may often be about things not important to you but of great importance to them. Sometimes you can resolve such issues with a few telephone calls or emails only the Chair can make. Such matters may have little consequence, but you should still attend to them.

Of even greater importance, you and the dean may not agree on what matters are most significant and should be given precedence at any specific moment. Identifying the importance of particular responsibilities is a proxy for determining the amount of time and energy that should be spent on them. If you and a dean agree on the status of possible problems or conflict areas, you may find it relatively easy to develop a productive relationship. Even moderate disagreements are unlikely to cause significant disruption and may be ironed out in the regular give-and-take of administrative life. But if there are vast discrepancies in which either of you perceives a specific matter to be of primary importance while the other considers it trivial, further action is required.

The first step is a candid discussion with the dean to test your assumptions about her views. It may turn out that the discrepancy is due to a misunderstanding on either part and is less significant than you had thought. However, a candid discussion may also confirm your belief that the differences are substantial enough that they are likely to disrupt your relationship.

If this is so, the second step is to reconcile the differences. It may require some bargaining (i.e., I will give greater attention to the matter you consider essential if you agree to support my issue.) It may require both of you to agree to bring in a neutral and mutually agreeable third party to bridge differences or the intervention of someone senior to both of you in the management hierarchy. When you and the dean strongly disagree on whether you should focus (for example) on personnel development, or budgeting and planning, neither the department nor the college will be served appropriately. But when you and the dean approach such issues collaboratively, recognizing that your successes are collectively linked (and with a little bit of luck), a mutually acceptable resolution should be possible.

If the differences prove impossible to reconcile despite your best efforts, then the dean's judgment must be given precedence over yours as a matter of management hierarchy. You can consider the following options as step three: attempt continued persuasion over time, learn to live with the difference, or quit the Chair position. (Note of caution: do not threaten to leave unless you are prepared to do so or be removed by the dean).

Your Life as an Accidental Manager

The secret to being a good manager is that there *is* no secret. You can be effective even without elaborate training or the mastery of advanced professional skills if you are reasonably well-organized and remember notions of responsibility, acceptable behavior, and common sense that almost all of us are taught as we grow up. First-level academic management in higher education is simple enough so that practically anyone with a professional appointment at a college is bright enough, and the majority have a personality acceptable enough to do it. Managing a department is not rocket science. Success depends on your desire to serve, a predisposition for stick-to-it-iveness, a moderate tolerance for ambiguity, and a willingness to do the job. Although you may occasionally encounter a technical or complex matter for which you may feel unprepared, most colleges employ experienced attorneys, accountants, computer technicians, and other experts you can use on an as-needed basis.

You are likely to spend more than half your time on managerial matters, although you will likely find these activities among your least satisfying (Gmelch & Miskin1995). What individual Chairs do depends on the type of program with which they are associated, the characteristics of the individuals within their department, institutional policies, history, and previous practices that have been affected by institutional culture, timing, and luck – good or bad. Many Chairs are only reactive and respond only to the demands of senior administrators. But it is also possible to manage proactively, for example, by studying how comparable programs at similar institutions are funded and staffed, by researching the effects of alternate enrollment policies, or by carefully reading the faculty development literature - and then advocating best practices in the department. You can often use such information to press for the approval of department financial or programmatic requests and occasionally inform department and college policy. You will be expected to perform many tasks for which you have not been adequately prepared. Developing a budget or an annual report can be a mysterious and painful experience for a newbie Chair.

Chairs who are accidental managers frequently learn by trial and error – that is, by acting based on their 'gut feeling' and then responding to the feedback they get. However, you can also learn by seeking the counsel of other more experienced Chairs. You can turn for advice to the department's long-time administrative assistant (if you are lucky enough to have one), consult with the dean or the dean's executive assistant, or talk with your experienced department members, including a former Chair if there is one.

One managerial responsibility that is almost universal among Chairs, which generally calls for consultation with other Chairs and with the dean's office, is preparing the annual department budget. A budget is the department's program presented in financial terms. A successful document ties the request for resources to department strategy and institutional goals and objectives. You must prepare and submit these critical financial documents in specified formats using uniform definitions. Successful completion of budget requests without requiring additional reworking by other college officials is essential if a college is to operate smoothly and efficiently. If a department budget document is prepared in a slip-shod manner that requires intervention and correction by other administrators, you may lose the dean's confidence. If a budget is prepared that doesn't reflect the department's interests, you may lose the confidence of department members. You should become quickly and intimately familiar with how department and college budgets are formatted and formulated and the deadlines that have been set. You should learn whether and under what circumstances additional items may be included or exceptions made and how budget allocations have changed over time. Some Chairs prepare budgets that emphasize the document's structure with little concern for content; others may prepare budgets that emphasize program elements with little regard for structure and format. Both approaches are mistaken.

Wise Chairs usually begin their term of office by following the management procedures accepted and understood by everyone in the past. If necessary, you can try slowly to change undesirable aspects. Unwise Chairs may begin by quickly making what they perceive as obviously (to them) needed changes, often without adequate consultation. The advice provided by a snake charmer to new students might be offered to newly appointed Chairs as well: "Don't make any sudden or unexpected moves."

Meetings and Decision-Making

Colleges are run through their meetings, and one of your most critical responsibilities will be to make meetings as productive as possible. Meetings are helpful when they allow people to share information, make announcements, or engage in group decision-making. But meetings can be detrimental if used to create obstacles for others, display status or power, or support work avoidance by substituting discussion for action.

The way to avoid this is for you to ensure that everyone in your department "thoroughly and completely" understands the problem, knows the requirements for an acceptable choice, helps in developing a list of alternatives, and assesses both the positive and negative consequences of each option (Hollingshead et al. 2005). These are valuable theoretical suggestions, but the chances that most academic departments will follow them are close to zero, as anyone who has worked in a college knows.

Since the department is unlikely to do these things, you, as Chair, should do so as a homework assignment before the meeting. Follow as many of these recommendations as possible and insert what you know into the discussion. You should pay particular attention to having the department consider as many alternatives as possible (many of which will probably come from you) since anything not mentioned during this stage is unlikely to be thought of later when a decision is made. Remember that many academic problems are "evaluative, behavioral or aesthetic…for which there is no correct solution" (p. 28). You are unlikely to develop a rational 'best' solution for such problems, and reaching a consensus is as much as you can expect. At the same time, you must avoid 'groupthink,' which can develop when everyone likes everyone else, and members won't challenge each other. Preventing groupthink may require you to serve as 'devil's advocate' to provoke more analytic discussion.

It has been suggested (Simon 1947) that people who share the same facts and values will make the same rational decision when faced with a problem. The operational word here is 'rational'; we know from behavioral economics that decision-making is replete with biases and heuristics that compromise rationality. Nevertheless, even if complete rationality is impossible, one purpose of meeting as a group is to share information so that all members are singing from the same hymnal. If valid information is shared, the possibility increases that participants will be less likely to engage in fantasy because they have been grounded in reality. Another purpose is to share values through open discussion and attempts to influence each other. Both processes should minimize conflict and disagreement caused by differences in group members' perceptions of problems and potential solutions. Rational decisions may still be hard to come by since, as we now know, human thought processes are rife with unconscious and irrational elements. Even (particularly?) minor differences can lead to significant disagreements. As has been said, academic fights are so bitter because the stakes are so small!

Rather than making decisions by voting, which can create winners and losers, you can try decision-making by consensus after a thorough and open discussion. Consensus doesn't mean complete agreement by all members of the group. Consensus is reached when most group members agree, those who don't are willing to accept it and give it a fair trial, and no one is intensely opposed.

You can use decision-making by consensus when the problems being addressed are non-routine and have no pressing time constraints. It helps when the group has expertise diffused among its members, no single person has all the data, group norms encourage openness, the group has prior experience in reaching consensus, and group members expect to be involved. Developing a department's five-year strategic plan would be an example.

Of course, these conditions do not apply to all departments or problems, and sometimes unilateral decision-making by the Chair is advisable and often acceptable to department members. This may be true when the issue is technical and a mutually agreed-on expert is available. Decision-making without consultation may be justified when all the data are known, there is a crisis and speed is essential, the problem is routine, and the group expects the Chair to decide. Deciding what color to paint the departmental meeting room would be an example. Unfortunately, some department members may believe that even paint color is critical to academic life and requires further assessment and consultation. One way to deal with such situations is to do what has to be done before anyone knows about it and let the discontents squabble about a <u>fait accompli</u>.

Whether you decide on your own or accept the group's consensus, you must remember that while you can delegate your authority to your colleagues, you cannot delegate your legal responsibility. Regardless of how the decision was made, it belongs to you. You alone are accountable for it, and its consequences, good or bad, rest on your shoulders.

Managing the Department Meeting

Although your responsibilities as Chair may vary widely, one required activity is almost certain; you will be expected to serve on many college committees and chair many of them within the department. This makes the ability to influence committee processes a particularly salient skill. Sometimes committees may be an annoyance. But in the meeting-rich environment of academic institutions, you can use your reliance on committees to your advantage. Meetings can reinforce educational values, strengthen members' influence on colleagues, focus the group's attention on significant issues, and encourage department members to collaborate collegially and constructively.

.   The major problem with committee effectiveness is usually not the topics they consider but the processes they follow. Without proper management, meetings can become circular, time-wasting, and irrelevant discussion forums that may not arrive at sensible conclusions. The tendency for faculty to discuss a matter endlessly is as natural today as it was over 100 years ago when one analyst (Slosson 1910, pp. 520-521) parodied it:

Order of Business at faculty meetings: Present motion. 2. Pass it. 3. Discuss it. 4. Reconsider it. 5. Amend it. 6. Amend the amendment. 7. Discuss it. 8. Move to lay on the table. 9. Discuss it. 10. Refer to a committee with power to act. 11. Discuss it. 12. Adjourn. 13 Discuss it.

At least, I think it was a parody!

An effective Chair understands that committees are forums where core academic principles of faculty authority, shared governance, and collegiality can be reinforced. What may be less obvious is that managing a meeting provides an unusual opportunity for you to exercise influence. Not just anyone can call a meeting, and your ability to do so reinforces your managerial authority. Presiding over a meeting gives you access to other unobtrusive levers of power as well because, as Chair, you can: determine when, where, and under what conditions a meeting is held; decide who shall attend; prepare the agenda; select where on the agenda any specific item will be placed; choose the order in which various participants are recognized to speak; initiate action; keep and distribute minutes; focus the discussion; call people out of order; and decide when the meeting should be ended. Moreover, unless you are seen as fulfilling these responsibilities arbitrarily or capriciously, they are an expected part of your managerial role and are unlikely to create resentment among department members.

Managing an effective meeting requires attending to the committee process at four different periods: before the meeting, during the meeting, after the meeting, and before the next meeting.

Before the Meeting. You should send a written reminder to department members of the time (beginning and ending) and the meeting place. You should distribute the written meeting agenda and attachments to members at least 24 hours in advance and provide necessary background information. In preparing the agenda, you should separate items that require discussion from those that are routine and for information only.

During the Meeting. You should start the meeting at the notified time and not wait for stragglers to arrive. Begin by reminding members of the meeting's purpose, requesting approval of the previous meeting minutes, and providing a brief opportunity for questions or corrections. When the group decides that some item is to be studied, you should specify who is to prepare the report and when it will be due (with this information included in the written minutes). You should ensure that everyone can participate during the meeting and let members occasionally control the discussion (as when a report is given). Your ability to ensure participation by everyone is essential because otherwise, higher-status members are likely to participate more and lower-status less, or not at all. As Chair, it is up to you to intervene as necessary so that everyone at the meeting has a voice (Hollingshead et al. 2005). You are always responsible for avoiding distractions, keeping the conversation on track, and remaining focused on the matter at hand.

At the End of the Meeting. You should review who has agreed to do what and when in the future, remind members of the next meeting's purpose, and solicit agenda items from the group. You should promptly end the meeting at the scheduled time so others can plan their other activities.

Before the Next Meeting. You should prepare and distribute the minutes of the last meeting, so that past discussions don't have to be repeated. (Distributing the minutes is mandatory; avoiding past discussions may be wishful thinking). You should also circulate those incoming materials that don't require discussion and do not need to be placed on the agenda. Preparing the minutes allows you to reinforce a desired narrative by stressing some items while minimizing others and reducing ambiguities in the meeting's outcomes.

To be effective, you should remind the department of timeliness and demonstrate this through example by always being punctual. You can poll members beforehand and select a meeting time acceptable to everyone to make attendance possible. The problem of full participation is not merely a matter of being efficient but also effective. Members who arrive at a meeting late or who leave early miss parts of the discussion. They cannot have a comprehensive view of what has been discussed, the data that has been presented, or the values that have been expressed.

Following these management practices will increase the likelihood that a meeting will efficiently use the participants' time, focus attention on a specific purpose, minimize distractions, and develop members' organizational skills. Ignoring these practices will likely lead to incoherent discussions that veer off-target and accomplish little.

One problem in department meetings is ensuring that everyone has an opportunity to be heard. Not only does the time available for overt communications decrease as the size of the group increases, but so does the distribution of communications (Hare 1962: 231-239). The gap in speaking time and attempts to influence between the top participators and others grows, fewer acts are initiated, and consensus becomes more difficult. One way of increasing individual participation is to use sub-committees; the smaller size of the new group may make agreement easier. A sub-committee report can frame the issue to the full committee meeting and provide a more stable core around which discussion may be held.

Recent college experiences using electronic media have permitted people to gather on Zoom or Facetime applications without being in physical contact. You may have to conduct some department meetings in the future online rather than in person. The implications of this possibility will not be understood until there has been more experience and analysis of its use. Holding unassembled meetings may have little effect on academic life. But it is also possible that such processes may increase administrative power and strain or even break the bonds of collegiality and participation that have traditionally defined the department as a unique entity. Your role may remain the same but may have to be enacted differently and in unforeseen ways.

Regardless of how the process may change, it will remain true that being a good committee member – listening with an open mind, exposing one's arguments to the scrutiny of others, and being as informed as possible – will continue to be as important as being a good Chair.

Perhaps the primary rule will remain the simplest for all committee members: Be There in person or online.

Management Made (Relatively) Simple

> *Administration ...is an uncodified art. Therefore, the only sure way to learn administration is to administer.* (Ashby 1962.276)

> *Habits are formed by action. The way to become a good administrator is to administer. But this is also the way* to become a bad administrator, for vice is a habit too. (Hutchins, 1946, p. 397).

As the quotations above suggest, learning management by doing is a two-edged sword. Fortunately, while requiring flexible attention to many changing issues, you can probably do the job if you want to, as long as you remember that

> *the daily activities of a manager are rather distinct from grand conceptions or organizational leadership. Administrators spend time talking to people about minor things, making trivial decisions, holding meetings with unimportant agendas, and responding to the little irritants of organizational life* (March 1984:16).

. Chairs are managers who make life easier for their colleagues by doing what must be done for the department without micromanaging faculty behavior. A good Chair minimizes hassles for others, establishes procedures to facilitate communication, corrects misinformation, buffers the unit from potential threats, and gives the group a sense of direction.

Here are my suggestions for good managerial practices for Chairs. Each suggestion is simple and easy to follow – but each is easy to ignore or forget when you are tired, under pressure, or feel overloaded or overwhelmed and think you are about to 'lose it.' Following these suggestions will place a more significant burden on your character than on your intellect. As you look at each proposal, think about what it might mean and consider whether it is something you should consider. You are likely to think of other desirable practices instead of, or in addition to, these. Good for you, but be sure you can articulate some conceptual or practical reasons for them.

Be Responsive. We have all had the frustrating experience of not receiving a response to a written or oral request for assistance or information or being told (misleadingly, as it often turns out), "I'll call you tomorrow." You should set an example of responsiveness. Answer your email and snail-mail within 24 hours. Return telephone calls promptly. Always be on time. Keep your promises. Colleagues may emulate Chairs when your behavior exemplifies professional responsibility and common courtesy. Your responsiveness will demonstrate your respect for those with whom you communicate. Your regularity and predictability will show that you are reliable and trustworthy.

Follow Appropriate Processes. Your department colleagues may be apathetic about many substantive issues because, in a college, most people are not concerned about most issues most of the time. But academics will almost certainly consider the process because it affects their right to participate in governance. In general, academics base their perceptions of legitimacy on how a policy was developed rather than its outcomes. You should follow accepted processes; the right way to do something is usually how department members expect it to be done.

Know the Rules. Every college has tons of policies that may affect members of your department. No group member can be familiar with all of them, but you must learn what they are and how they can be waived or altered. If there is a Board of Trustees policy manual or a compilation of institutional regulations, read them carefully. Being able to respond authoritatively to department members' questions reinforces your authority as an official. It confirms their perception of your expertise and makes it less likely that the members will act on incorrect information that will create problems later for themselves (and you).

De-emphasize Bureaucracy. Many academics depreciate the value of bureaucratic structures and offices and the officials who occupy them. Their dislike is strong enough that those seen as bureaucratic often cannot be seen differently. An emphasis on bureaucracy can reinforce dominance and become self-perpetuating. Department members become more likely to think of you as a 'boss' and less likely to see you as a colleague. Rather than just telling them a rule, remind them why the rule exists and why it ultimately serves their best interests. Never try to justify your right to make a decision "because I'm the Chair." If you do, you may win the battle, but the cost may be so high that you will lose the war.

Never give an Order that Will Not Be Obeyed. As Chair, you will soon learn how far you can go in asking one or more department members to do something. If your request is within their zone of acceptance (if it lies within the range of activities to which the faculty are indifferent and likely to follow without judgment), they will likely comply. But they are likely to object and defy you if it is outside that zone. Others in the department will recognize that you cannot get your way, and your ability to influence them in the future will therefore diminish.

Allocate Resources Fairly. Fairness is based less on the fairness of outcomes than the fairness of the procedures by which the results were developed (Lind & Tyler 1988). A need for fairness is a human universal with genetic origins, so you need to be aware of equity principles and the concept of distributive justice. Remember that "those who feel unjustly treated are likely to be belligerent" (Hollander 1978:8). Fairness in allocating tangible and fiscal resources comes most readily to mind, but don't overlook the allocation of some of the more critical intangible resources available to you as Chair. Giving individual group members your time, attention, support, or recognition, and treating them in a dignified way, are virtually unlimited rewards to which you have access. Humans instinctively recognize and dislike injustice. You should never give preferential treatment to a department member that others might consider unfair or inequitable. Treat group members equally (including – and perhaps particularly - those you don't care for); academics are quick to spot favoritism and impute (often impure) motives.

Don't Take it Personally. Some department members may see many decisions that appear to be trivial to you as very important. Others may consider almost any action you take to attack unit prerogatives to which they must respond. A Chair is a convenient lightning rod and scapegoat, so get used to it. Some Chairs have remarked that serving in that position is like being nibbled to death by ducks. You may begin to take these constant and annoying nibbles as personal attacks, but they are only what ducks do to pass the time and make themselves feel important. Sometimes merely smoothing their ruffled feathers can do wonders. Group members can sometimes make a Chair's life so miserable that you may be tempted to strike back. Please don't do it! Group members will recognize and commiserate with your suffering, but they may switch to taking the miscreant's side if you overreact. Don't use a bomb to kill a gnat – or a duck!

Explain Your Reasons. Managers are presumed to be rational. They do action 'A' because they believe it is most likely to lead to the desired outcome 'B.' Group members are more likely to have faith in you and be swayed by your arguments when they can understand why you are doing 'A' and why 'B' is desirable. Levels of trust within a department increase as its members learn that you are thoughtful and do not act arbitrarily or capriciously. In turn, group members are less likely to oppose understandable initiatives, even if they disagree.

Focus Attention. Budgets may decline, and public support decrease. The dean may not be enamored with your department. The college's budget formula may be unfair. The computer system may go down an hour before your report to the dean is due. None of these events are reasons for you to pass the buck or point fingers. Playing the blame game just avoids working on problems. Instead, you should refocus the group's attention, tell them, "this is what has happened, and this is where we are," and then ask, "given this, what should we do now to achieve our mission?"

Treat Your Staff Like Gold. Chairs may (but often don't) have one or more staff people such as secretaries, administrative assistants, IT folks, or typists who do administrative work. They occupy some of the lowest rungs of the hierarchical college ladder and do their jobs regardless of who the Chair happens to be. They are the people who make the department run smoothly. When treated like indispensable unit members, they may become part of a team that identifies with the department's mission and is ready to go the extra mile. People in these roles are often well-known to others in the college bureaucracy and, unbeknownst to you, may be very influential. Remember that department members may view them as even more crucial to the unit's success than the Chair – and often more difficult to replace!

Unfortunately, it is also possible that you have inherited an irresponsible employee who, despite frequent warnings, distributes incorrect data, loses files, forgets to take telephone messages, is unhelpful to students, and repeatedly misunderstands policies and procedures. Firing such a person is possible in some institutions, and the quicker, the better. However, if you are in an institution whose classified staff members are civil service employees or belong to a union, I weep for you, my friend. Efforts to dismiss a staff member under these circumstances often require such elaborate documentation and procedures that removing them from their positions is virtually impossible. What can you do? Write a memo to the miscreant after each error or violation, with a copy to the college personnel office for the employee's file and a copy to the employee. Follow this with (yet another) personal meeting with you to deliver an admonishment. It's not much, to be sure, but at least you will have the satisfaction of trying.

Assume Ignorance Rather Than Malice in Others. It is easy – perhaps even natural – to assume that when some people disagree with you, they are motivated by troubled personalities or self-interests. In some cases, this may be true. But when disagreements arise, it is better to assume instead (at least initially) that they stem from a misunderstanding rather than evil intent. Investigate the reasons for your disagreement before making assumptions that may soon become self-fulfilling prophecies. The dean may not be the jerk you think he is but is acting based on more information than is available to you. A colleague may be annoyed with you simply because, like many academics, she is unaware of some college processes you are legally obliged to follow. You can correct ignorance, but malice tends to be self-perpetuating.

Prepare for Your Departure. Because of the uncertainties and ambiguities of the position, there may come a time when you want to leave the Chair, or the dean has made it very clear that she wants you gone. These possibilities mean that you should consider becoming a Chair only if you are a full professor with tenure. Pressure on a Chair with only an administrative term appointment or a promotion pending can be overwhelming, irresistible, and threaten your career and livelihood. You may be subject to an order from the dean that you think would be immoral to carry out, or you may be no longer willing to tolerate undesirable conflict related to your 'being in the middle.' When the wheels are coming off the cart, having tenure is the 'go to hell' card that will allow you to have agency over your situation and preserve your academic integrity.

It's O.K. to be an Academic Manager

Some academics consider 'administration' and 'management' dirty words. They are not. Administrators who manage are essential in large, complex organizations such as colleges to provide the organization, data, information, and direction required for coordinated behavior. Being a good manager is often a first step to being a good leader, but they are not the same. Fortunately, Chairs who are primarily managers can positively influence their departments even if they are not leaders.

Accept an appointment as Chair with your eyes open. The position has many advantages, but there is also the possibility that serving as a Chair may not have a successful outcome. Listening carefully to colleagues, being patient, and gracefully accepting the minor inconveniences of the role appear to be among the attributes that promote a positive and productive tenure as Chair.

The idiosyncratic nature of what Chairs do means that there is no specific type of person, and no particular skills, that are uniquely required to provide successful departmental management. Even though Chair candidates may have diverse backgrounds and experiences and take the position for various reasons, quite different people can do the job well. You may be one of them.

Chapter Three

Academic Leadership

To be a lone chief atop a pyramid is abnormal and corrupting...When someone is moved atop a pyramid, that person no longer has colleagues, only subordinates. (Greenleaf 1977: 63)

'Leadership' is, at the same time, both the simplest and the most complex human activity. Leadership exists in every social group of two or more people because a leadership structure always appears whenever people work together (Hollander 1978). As soon as a relationship or group forms, no matter how informal, a pattern of authority is created that establishes "the distribution of responsibilities, duties, needs, expectations, privileges and rewards" (Nesbitt & Perrin 1977: 106). There is no such thing as a group without a leader since a group structure creates a leadership structure. Leadership is an interaction based on mutual influence, and the term 'leader' refers to a group member who influences more frequently or persistently than other group members (Gibb 1969:11).

Remember that influence can be non-coercive (leadership) or coercive (domination). Willing followers create leaders. Dominants don't have followers. They have underlings, subjects, submissives, flunkies, and all those 'little people' who, when you think about it, are the folks who make the college work. If they want to.

This means that leadership can only be understood by incorporating the concept of followership, which is why this book for department Chairs emphasizes the expectations of the department members who may be your followers. You may try to initiate action as Chair, but success requires that followers accept your attempted influence. Trying to understand leadership by focusing solely on the Chair as a department leader is an exercise in futility. As scholars (Kouzes & Posner 2003:1) have pointed out, "strategies, tactics, skills, and practices are empty unless we understand the fundamental human aspirations that connect leaders and their constituents." It's the connection – the interaction – that matters.

When you are seen as influential, your social status increases, and you may obtain increased resources and other rewards. Less obvious is why your colleagues would accept your influence. A simple reason may be that it is in their individual best interest. Allowing you to influence them reduces their need to expend energy and decreases their need to question everything, no matter how minor. They will accept your influence if you have demonstrated your expertise in the past and have been right most of the time. But, as we shall see, there are more complex reasons as well.

Leadership and Followership

Leadership and followership are not mutually exclusive but support each other. In one situation, you as Chair may realize the greater competence of, and agree to be guided by, a colleague. In another, the relationship may be reversed. You do not lose your status or independence by being a voluntary follower. By accepting the leadership of others some of the time, you strengthen the social bonds and norms that make it easier for them to accept your leadership most of the time. When you demonstrate a commitment to group norms by responding to the leadership of others, it increases your ability to lead.

Leadership is an art, more than a science. It often depends on judgment, intuition, and experience, even more than analysis and 'facts.' As with any art, almost anyone can develop some measure of leadership proficiency. However, some will be much better at it than others. Leadership in a department can be exercised by many people who hold no formal office ('informal leadership'). However, I want to focus on how leadership can be developed in departments and other relatively small academic groups by those appointed to specific positions of authority, such as department Chairs ('formal leadership').

What do Leaders Do?

All Chairs must be managers, but only some become leaders. Managers who become leaders are likely to come from the small proportion of Chairs I identified earlier as 'exemplary.' I am unaware of any studies that have assessed Chairs using these average/exemplary/failed categories. However, research has considered college presidents this way (Birnbaum 1992). I think it is reasonable to assume that the relative performance of

Chairs is similar because these three categories approximate a normal distribution. Like most other aspects of life, leadership capabilities are likely distributed normally. If Chairs follow the patterns of presidents, about half of all department Chairs would be average, and a quarter would fail. That leaves only about one-quarter of department Chairs who would be exemplary, and these are the Chairs most likely to be identified as leaders.

What do exemplary department Chairs do when they become leaders? They help the department clarify and become committed to agreed-upon purposes. They support the autonomy of department members. They help reduce uncertainty by defining confusing situations and conveying new meanings. They facilitate cooperation within the department and between the department and other groups. They give their members a sense of group 'belongingness'. They influence how their followers interpret reality, and they focus followers' attention on what is important. They enforce group norms, manage conflict, ensure the fair distribution of resources, maintain the social order, attend to internal and environmental issues, model behavior, and provide safety and security. They try to make the department self-policing so that members other than the Chair can correct errant behavior, and 'free-riders' (those who benefit from group membership but don't contribute) are not tolerated. Chairs as leaders protect the department's continuity by helping its members develop both leadership and followership skills.

As a Chair and a potential leader, you may be tempted to throw up your hands after reviewing these leadership responsibilities (which, of course, are in addition to those you must perform as a manager). Fortunately, you don't have to be a superhero and do all these things all the time to be a leader. Instead, you have to discover which of these behaviors your group wants and needs. Management tasks do not interfere with leadership but instead provide perfect situations where the Chair's leadership can be exhibited.

Managers and leaders share many commonalities. Distinguishing between them in a college is often pointless because proposals that strengthen one often enhance the other. Take, for example, the development of a department's strategic plan. Determining its structure, timing, and degree of member participation and then preparing the final document and moving it through the appropriate governance bodies for approval may be called 'management.' Helping the department come to grips with critical problems, and finding solutions that engage group members and support the institution's goals, might be called 'leadership.' Both processes use pretty similar ideas. And whether considered management or leadership, a department works best when you, as Chair, are seen as honest, moral, impartial, fair, responsible, and accountable. In other words, you should be a good person.

Academic management and academic leadership often involve the same people engaging in similar behaviors. The significant difference between them is the sources of their authority. Department managers have legal authority delegated to them from the management hierarchy superior to the unit. In contrast, a department leader has the professional and moral authority that only department members themselves can grant.

Being formally appointed as an official by the college hierarchy identifies you as a manager but cannot by itself make you a leader. The mantle of leadership is more likely to be conferred on you by the members of your department if you possess expertise and likeability and do not alienate the group. You must demonstrate at least some personal charisma or engage in charisma-like behaviors, help the group in adaptive problem-solving, and identify something you wish to achieve that would improve group performance. Merely holding an official position such as Chair and issuing commands do not make you a leader; they make you a manager.

You may become a leader if you can produce and equitably distribute the benefits your followers expect. If you cannot fulfill your followers' expectations, you must change them in a manner the department deems appropriate. Leaders provide the means of achieving the followers' goals (Gibb 1969), and leadership is constrained in every organization and level. Your leadership is constrained by what your followers permit.

You can always influence your department as Chair because of the authority delegated to you in your official managerial position (the charisma of office). But if department members have also identified you as a leader because of personal characteristics (the charisma of person), you will gain a vast increment of authority. Later we will examine the kinds of social power that Chairs have available and show how the sources of management influence differ from those of leadership influence.

Selecting a Group Leader

To be accepted, leaders must be selected by their groups, and groups initially use three criteria to identify potential leaders. These criteria, which have roots in both biology and culture, have been consistently applied by human groups for thousands of years in many settings. If you want to be considered a leader, your department must agree that you have met three requirements.

First, you must be selected legitimately. Because it involves some semblance of individual choice and control, leaders elected by followers are more likely to be considered legitimate than those appointed by those higher in the social structure. Elected leaders, whose influence is more likely dependent on personal persuasion than the coercive authority of office, are also likely to have more responsive followers (Hollander 1985).

The actual selection process is less critical to the department's acceptance than the perception that the correct procedures were followed. What are the correct procedures? They are whatever processes the department expects and accepts. Many academic departments expect to elect their Chair or be consulted before a Chair is named. In contrast, some academic departments are content to let a dean make the judgment. No matter how unusual, any process is acceptable as long as it is considered by the group to be legitimate. Before accepting a Chair position, it would be wise for you to talk to department members and ensure that they believe your selection procedure is acceptable. If you are not selected by accepted practices, you may not be considered legitimate by the group and would, therefore, be at risk of failing even before you start.

Second, you must be seen to adhere to and support the department's values. Different academic groups have different values. Some prize teaching; others give precedence to the possession of technical skills, the creation of knowledge, diversity, community service, or career preparation. You will only be considered a leader if you are seen as committed to the department's ideals, whatever those might happen to be. If you are known as a distinguished researcher and appointed as Chair of a department that values teaching, you might not be seen as sharing the group's values and would be at risk of failing.

Third, you must possess some expertise that is important to the group. Your department will anticipate you will have enough knowledge of their academic and professional fields to understand, value, and defend what the group members do. But they also want you to bring some particular expertise that the group needs and values. You could demonstrate that expertise if your appointment brings additional recognition and acclaim to a department. You might also show it by visibly establishing valuable personal relationships with senior officials, diversifying the faculty's concepts and views, securing external funding, exhibiting state-of-the-art knowledge of some technology, or developing new programs. Only the group itself can assess the nature of the expertise they consider at the time to be necessary. If you are not seen as having the type of expertise the group is looking for, you are at risk of failing.

When groups select leaders, they are more likely to pay attention to whether a Chair candidate conforms to group norms than whether the candidate exhibits stereotypical administrative characteristics (Hollingshead et al. 2005). If legitimacy, values, and expertise are present, becoming a group's leader is possible but not guaranteed. Suppose any of these three things are not present. In that case, it is virtually impossible to be accepted as a leader by a group because it is the group, and neither you nor any other college authority, that determines whether or not these criteria have been met. Different groups will define these criteria differently and at different times, so leadership is situation-specific. Being a leader in one situation does not necessarily transfer to another, even if the conditions may superficially appear identical.

The criteria for group leadership are not necessarily related to a college's definitions of quality of performance, efficient operation, consistency with institutional values, or any other standard, academic or otherwise. The department determines the criteria. Followers may accept a Chair's attempt at influence, or they may not. But leaders can only go where followers will let them.

The Fair Exchange

It's good to be a leader! Leaders gain increased prestige, reap economic benefits, and find the group's willingness to respond to their influence personally rewarding. Leaders are even helped by biochemistry; levels of testosterone (for dominance) and serotonin (for happiness) rise when someone acquires power, and "leaders start to radiate confidence and energy. They become more attractive" (Nicholson 2000:116). So leaders get a lot. But group members also benefit when they willingly accept the influence of a leader. Having a leader relieves the group of dealing personally with many of the college hierarchies' demands. Department members can preserve their time and energy when they authorize the leader to represent their interests. When a group selects a leader who shares their values, they can trust the leader to respond to issues and problems as they would themselves. That's why groups are often more likely to accept an elected official's behaviors than those of an appointed one.

With the acceptance of a leader, the group implicitly enters into a psychological contract with the leader for what has been called (Hollander 1978) "a fair exchange." The presumption of a fair exchange is tacit, but if it were ever written down, the contract with the leader, as seen by any group member, might have two clauses that look something like this:

The first clause:

I am willing to support your position of authority, accept without complaint that you have a higher salary and other perquisites not available to me, cede to you some (but not all) of my professional autonomy, and respond positively to your initiatives. I do so because I want you to succeed, and I recognize that your success will also make me successful. I helped to select you, so I know that you share my values, that you will serve my interests, and that you will protect me. Knowing you are my leader increases my self-esteem and makes it more likely that I will achieve my own goals. Also, I enjoy working with you and like to be personally associated with you. I know you are not perfect, and I'll forgive you if you occasionally fail, just as I'm sure you will forgive me if I sometimes screw up because you are one of us.

The second clause:

But if you slack off, if you regularly fail in the future to meet my expectations, if the benefits I anticipated because of your expertise don't materialize, or if you begin to give more attention to your interests than to mine, then the exchange between us is no longer fair, and our implicit leader-follower contract is null and void. If that happens, I will withdraw my willingness to be influenced by you, and you will become only a manager with limited power to enforce rules and policies.

A fair exchange suggests that a group is willing to be influenced by its acknowledged leader, which implies that there is something you want to achieve. You will find it challenging to implement new initiatives, and the more managerial effort and authority you use to do so, the less likely it is that you will succeed. Purposefully creating new group values is difficult, if not impossible (at least in the short term). And even the best group members can find their ideals swamped by the constant need to attend to the daily problems of college life. But a fair exchange agreement gives you the license to try to implement new ideas.

Leader-centric or Group-centric?

One fundamental way of thinking about leadership is whether it is leader-centric or group-centric. The leader-centric view puts you, as Chair, front and center and emphasizes your influence and acumen in determining and achieving goals for the group. If you are leader-centric, you believe you should make decisions and solve group problems. You think a formal leader should direct the group's activities, make decisions, get them accepted by group members, and convince them to follow your vision. In this view, leaders should make difficult decisions about group purposes and activities, identify and correct group members' mistakes, and determine the group's strategy and core goals.

On the other hand, the group-centered view emphasizes having the department determine and achieve its own goals while you provide assistance and support as necessary. From this perspective, you should help the group make essential decisions, understand group members' expectations, and motivate group members to achieve common goals. You should encourage department members to exercise initiative, raise their moral consciousness, coordinate group activities, and focus their attention on solving their problems.

All formal leaders face this fundamental philosophical choice of whether to direct or serve the group. There are no data available to suggest which approach is best. However, the expected norms and values of the academic world indicate that leaders should be more effective if their groups view them as facilitators rather than directors.

The concept of the group-oriented leader is sometimes difficult to accept. We are likely to think of leadership in terms of individual agency because of the human tendency to believe in the efficacy of personal action. Group success tends to be attributed to effective leadership, even when evidence suggests that leaders had little involvement. We want to believe that outcomes are caused by people rather than by chance or uncontrollable external forces. We also tend to blame group shortcomings on a failure of leadership instead of a failure of followership.

Both leader-centric and group-centric views can be problematic. Leaders who overemphasize their efficacy can often cause internal conflict. If you are self-focused, you may initially impress group members but then lose their support as it becomes evident that your interests are not consistent with theirs. Academic history is replete with accomplished and self-regarding individuals who, over time, become seen by others as autocratic and exploitative. On the other hand, some formal leaders who downplay their ability to initiate behavior can lose sight of their potential influence over time and, through their inactivity, allow a group to miss opportunities for improvement.

Regardless of the term used to describe it, research indicates that followers see good leaders as supportive, listening, clarifying goals and methods, results-oriented, a good delegator, and fair. Bad leaders are unsupportive and lack communication skills. They are seen as uninvolved, unfair, angry, harsh, autocratic, and poor managers of resources. In any case, it is almost certainly true that the leader who would succeed senses and delivers what an audience already desires (Gardner 1995).

Using Social Power

You will remember that Chairs, as officials, can influence their group because of 'charisma of office' created by their position in the college hierarchy. The Chair, content to be only a manager, can say, "I don't need to be liked, just respected." In contrast, a Chair who wishes to be a leader must have both 'charisma of office' and 'charisma of person.' I am not using this concept of personal charisma in its most fulsome "gift of grace" definition, but instead in its contemporary meaning, referring to someone admired and esteemed by department members. A leader must say, "I need to be both liked and respected."

While leadership is a form of influence, not all forms of influence can be called leadership. Why is it that leaders can do things that managers cannot? Why is it that being liked increases the potential to exert influence? Why can an official influence a group at one time but lose that ability later? You may find answers to these questions by understanding the positive and negative consequences of using different forms of social power.

Chairs can influence group members using one or a combination of five sources of social power (French & Raven 1959); coercive power, reward power, legitimate power, expert power, and referent power. Coercive physical power was probably the primary source of influence for prehistoric humans. We inherited from them the hard-wired genetic penchant for establishing a status hierarchy enforced by violent behavior. We also inherited from them the human insistence on independence and autonomy. The development of power alternatives in our culture suggests how you can influence your followers as Chair. The potential sources of your social power are:

Coercive Power. This power (do this or I will damage your reputation, exile you, fire you) influences group members to obey you as Chair because they believe they will be punished if they do not.

Reward Power. This power (do this, and you will get a salary increment, a strong letter of recommendation, membership on a high-status committee) influences group members to obey you as Chair because they believe they will be rewarded with something of value if they do.

Legitimate Power. This power influences group members to obey you as Chair because they believe that your position as an official in the college hierarchy gives you the right to make decisions and give orders.

Expert Power. This power influences group members to do what you as Chair ask because they realize you have more valid information and expertise about an issue than they do.

Referent Power. This power influences group members to do what you as Chair asks because they like, identify with, and are anxious to please you.

The Consequences of Using Power

Using any of the five sources of social power may lead members to comply. If this is so, why select one rather than another? The answer is that using different kinds of power usually has predictable outcomes. Your use of power may either please group members and increase your influence in the future or alienate the group members and lessen your future influence.

Coercion is a relative concept with many shades of meaning. One scholar (Greenleaf 1977:42) has said:

Some coercive power is overt and brutal. Some of it is covert and subtly manipulative. The former is open and acknowledged, the latter is insidious and hard to defeat. Most of us are more coerced than we know... Part of the dilemma is that all leadership is, to some extent, manipulative.

The problem differentiating between domination and leadership is that almost all forms of influence contain some coercive elements. Influence is rarely purely leadership or domination but usually falls between these two poles and includes both aspects. While some examples of coercion (such as putting a gun to your head) do not create leaders or willing followers, others are not clear-cut. Can making the availability of resources such as food or money conditional on accepting influence be considered an act of leadership? How about withdrawing signals of affection or approval? Or inserting a penalty clause into a contract or violating norms by boycotting a negotiating meeting? All are forms of coercion, yet some may be considered acts of leadership more than others, depending on the audience.

The gray areas of coercion suggest that leadership depends on the nature of the followers being considered and the specific nature of the influence involved. Domination offers one-way communication and the application of force to assure compliance. On the other hand, leadership is a dynamic process of two-way influence that involves both what leaders do and how engaged followers actively respond (Hollander 2006). Leadership is not something that is 'off' or 'on,' but rather something that is 'more' or 'less' at different times. Leadership involves mutually agreeable transactions among people whose social lives depend on their relationships with others (Fiske 1992:689). As we shall see later, the mechanisms that support both the ideas of domination and leadership have their biological roots in the evolution of the human species

The Consequences of Using Coercive Power. No one likes to be coerced or threatened. A department may do what you want if you threaten its members with physical, political, social, or financial retribution. But such coercion is also likely to cause fear, anger, and alienation. In other words, people get pissed off. Consequently, even if group members appear to agree with your demand, they may try to undermine it, follow the letter but not the spirit of a new policy, refuse to enact it when no one is watching them, or sabotage it. When your order is not obeyed, you lose influence, your status is diminished, and the department will be less willing to accept your influence in the future.

The Consequences of Using Reward Power. Some department members may be motivated by rewards such as salary improvements or promises of promotions or perquisites. If they are offered, they may become more productive. But many others find such rewards unprofessional and distasteful, and they may become alienated. Remember, academics are not primarily motivated by rewards like money. Doing something for a reward may reinforce the perception that the recipient is subservient to the person granting it. Significant financial rewards may spur activity, but college awards are often small, and discriminating among group members for, say, awarding annual performance increments, may prove divisive.

The Consequences of Using Legitimate Power. As Chair, you have a prescribed degree of legal authority and can exercise your office's legitimate power without generating favorable or unfavorable feelings among most department members. As long as you act within the bounds of normal and appropriate behavior, group members will likely be indifferent and accept what you say or do, thus increasing your future influence. However, you may create anger and alienation if you act outside the group's 'zone of acceptance.'

The Consequences of Using Expert Power. Expertise is highly valued, particularly among academics. Suppose your colleagues see you as having areas of expertise that the group recognizes as related to its success, such as having received a prestigious research award or being recognized as having created new teaching methodologies. In that case, they may see you as an expert, and you are more likely to influence them without inducing alienation when these matters are under discussion.

The Consequences of Using Referent Power. Group members are likely to give special attention to a Chair with whom they can identify and who has their respect and admiration. This referent power may be a response to your personal charisma or, to a lesser extent, your regular use of referent-like behaviors, such as remaining calm in a crisis, smiling and being friendly, and leading by example. Your use of referent power can exert influence without creating alienation. Expert and referent power are based on symbolic rewards, leading to commitment and an intensely positive reaction (Etzioni 1961).

All five forms of power are potentially available to you, and all can influence what groups do. But can all of them be used by someone wishing to be a leader? Influence based on threats to harm group members, promises to reward, or legitimate power outside the group's zone of acceptance reflects dominance rather than leadership. Dominance may induce group members to comply, but because it causes an intense negative response is also likely to alienate them. They may disobey you or stop behaving as you wish once the threat or promise is no longer available.

As a Chair, you may be able to use coercive, reward, and even legitimate power that the group dislikes to a limited extent in your manager role. Some Chairs may be clever enough to calculate how far they can go with them without inciting rebellion. But excessive use of coercive, reward, or even legitimate power may cause you to forfeit any possibility of being identified by the group as a leader. In contrast, Chairs who are thought of as leaders, try to influence their departments through expert and referent power. These two forms of power and the moderate and appropriate use of legitimate power within the group's zone of acceptance are generally non-threatening and non-alienating. Of course, expert or referent power must be earned before exercising these powers. You have a claim to a form of expertise because you will probably interact more with the dean and other high-level college officials, and you are likely to know more about institutional matters than your colleagues.

Both managers and leaders utilize the same sources of power. The differences between them may not be the social powers they use but the frequency with which they use them and the consequent impact on the group's willingness to accept influence in the future. Remember that leadership is both a science and an art. The science of leadership tells us that influence can be gained or lost depending on the extent to which each of the five sources of power has been, and is being, used. The art of leadership is that the proper mix of these five types of power cannot be prescribed but must be determined by each Chair who wishes to be identified as a leader by a specific group. How these five sources of power are used does not depend on what the Chair objectively does but rather on the group's perception of the Chair's appropriateness.

As Chair, you must always attend to the effects of these power sources. Using any particular form of power is not often manifest by your conscious decision to think, "I should use referent power on issue X, or legitimate power on issue Y," but by the habits of mind you will develop over time. These habits are related to groups' expectations in different organizational settings.

The ability to influence department members using non-alienating power depends on the group's beliefs. You may need time and consistent behavior to develop influence-based referent and expert power. However, always remember that this influence can be lost almost immediately through a single non-judicious act or use of coercion. Trust is not a symmetrical process: it can take years to gain it, but only a moment to lose it.

Leadership Made (Relatively) Simple

In Chapter Two, I proposed ten simple principles that would enable managers to be more effective. It is much more difficult to suggest simple principles for leadership because it is more complex, emphasizes an individual's ability to influence others' interpretations and perceptions, and depends on the reciprocal interaction between the leader and members of the group. Nevertheless, even if 'simple' leadership principles aren't possible, I can propose some 'relatively simple' leadership notions. They can be glibly stated in a few short words, but how they may be implemented (and sometimes even whether they should be attempted) in specific cases is a matter of individual judgment. Following these principles may not make you a leader, but they should make becoming a leader more likely.

Listen Carefully. Even if you hear what someone says, you may not understand what they mean. You are likely to listen carefully to your supporters, but it may be more important to listen carefully to those who disagree with you and explore their reasons. If leaders believe their role is to tell others what to do, they may not give proper attention to listening; if they don't listen, groups won't allow themselves to be influenced. If leaders don't listen to their groups, they won't understand their concerns or be able to help them.

Empower Others. A significant role of leadership is to develop the collective capacity of the group. The value of leadership is not necessarily a function of the qualities of a single person but depends on the density of informal leadership within the group. Dispersing leadership capabilities increases the group's strength by providing additional avenues to sense problems, monitor the environment, and think of alternative ways of approaching a problem.

Know Your Followers. Leaders are constrained by the limits imposed by the members of their group. The group may not follow through on a decision made solely by a formal leader, and when groups refuse to act, their leaders suffer a reduction in their status and influence. Dramatic, authoritative, and decisive leadership behavior may be counterproductive in an academic institution where groups expect participation.

Be Part of the Group. Regularly interact with group members, as a colleague rather than as an official, in both informal and formal settings. Suppose you know the people you regularly interact with and share their values. In that case, you are likely to have a good idea of what they want and what you should avoid doing because the group would find it distasteful and alienating. Exercise influence in unobtrusive ways and change group perceptions by choosing what you emphasize or de-emphasize.

Allow Yourself to be Influenced. Leadership is a process of interaction, and the price for influencing others is allowing yourself to be influenced. Leaders who are not believed to be responding to the influence of others are usually seen as acting unilaterally and are resented. Although it may appear that increasing the influence of others will result in decreasing your own, the reality is precisely the opposite. The influence pie is not a fixed size; enlarge it.

Articulate Values. Groups that focus too much attention on instrumental issues may lose sight of the fundamental ways in which a college differs from other organizations. Leaders should constantly remind the group of the transcendent values that brought them together in the first place. You can justify decisions in terms of consistency with these values or question inconsistent choices. These values should not be assumed but should constantly be articulated so they eventually can become internalized by the department.

Emphasize Strengths, not Weaknesses. Focusing on strengths indicates that the group is doing well and will do even better in the future. Emphasizing strengths can maintain or raise group morale, and these strengths can serve as a foundation for further growth and development. On the other hand, speaking of weaknesses is a constant reminder of unit problems and defects likely to reduce productivity and unit morale further. Highlighting weaknesses increases the possibility that individual group members may be identified as the weaknesses that should be removed.

Honor the Group's History and Traditions. Many academic groups have long histories of accomplishments, honors, or travails embedded in the collective memory of members. Other groups have traditions whose original purposes may have been lost in time but are still followed and revered. If you know and value what the group has done and what rituals are followed, you will have insight into what motivates your colleagues and are more likely to be seen as 'one of us.'

Have Modest Expectations. Within your first two weeks as Chair you will likely identify dozens of problems within your department, and you may have an impulse to fix them immediately. Resist that impulse! You are unlikely to know the reasons for these problems, and there are many ways in which minor issues can be interwoven with a major one. Start your official duties with careful watching, listening, and questioning before deciding to do anything. Then focus on a few primary objectives; if you try to accomplish too much, you may achieve nothing.

———————————————

In Chapters One, Two, and Three, I have discussed the Chair's role in college management and leadership. My analyses and suggestions are grounded in the work of scholars who have studied the effectiveness of small groups and the functions that leaders and followers play.

In Chapters Four, Five, and Six, we will be moving into new territory that, to my knowledge, has never before been used to consider leadership in higher education. These Chapters begin by providing some background descriptions of the interactions of biology and culture to suggest how they influenced the development of 'leadership' in the small, intimate, primordial human bands that existed 20,000 years ago. I will consider leadership in the small human groups of long ago to see how it compares to the suggestions of contemporary scholars and if it has any relevance to the leadership processes of Chairs today who are responsible for the functioning of a small departmental group.

Soon we will be considering leadership in the Stone Age. But first, a discussion of brains, genes, and memes – oh my!

Chapter Four

Leadership is All in Your Head: An Important Digression

Man with all his noble qualities, with sympathy for the most debased, with benevolence which extends not only to other men but to the humblest living creature, with his god-like intellect which has penetrated into the movements and constitution of the solar system – with all these exalted powers – Man still bears in his bodily frame the indelible stamp of his lowly origin. (Darwin 1871:21)

I mentioned earlier that leadership has both biological and cultural roots. The biological portion is in our genes; they have created a bodily frame, including a brain, that reveals the human inheritance from our apish ancestors. The cultural component is in our memes, a different form of inheritance that is uniquely human. How do these two forms of inheritance interact to affect leadership?

Genes and Leadership

It is romantic to think leadership comes from the heart or the gut. But the reality is that leadership comes from the brain. Because the brain constructs and controls all of our senses, thoughts, actions, and emotions, from the simplest to the most complex (Kandel 2006), it must also be the source of human leadership and followership behavior.

How does that happen, and what does it mean for you as a Chair? A discussion of the biology and culture of leadership may appear to be a digression. Still, it may help you understand how and why leadership has been transformed during human evolution and how it affects your influence today.

Brains

From the biggest to the smallest, the brains of all animals contain neurons that are connected – hard-wired - to each other. The pattern of hard-wiring is different for each species and is created by genes. The hard-wiring is innate (i.e., present at birth or reliably develops at certain ages) and permits and often requires the animal to behave in specific ways. As a simple example, consider the dung beetle. The dung beetle is a tiny animal, about one inch long, with a very small brain. It is 'born' with the hard-wired ability to smell feces and cut off a chunk. It then rolls the piece into a ball and pushes it in a straight line (guided by the stars!) away from other beetles that would like to steal it. Once the ball is safely away from potential rivals, the beetle eats it. Well, *chacun à son goût.* That's a pretty basic repertoire (although the 'star light' part is impressive), but cutting, rolling, eating, making other beetles, and repeating is about all the dung beetle does.

Like the dung beetle, humans also have the hard-wired ability to smell feces. But instead of finding the odor delightful, as the dung beetle does, our brains are hard-wired to find it disgusting because, over evolutionary time, feces have made us sick. Human hardwiring permits us to do many things other than smell feces, such as exercising and responding to leadership. As far as we know, dung beetles do not exhibit leadership (although some politicians make you wonder).

Different animals have different, inborn, hard-wired modules. Because of their specialized brains, bees can see things in the ultra-violet spectrum, dogs can smell chemicals, elephants can hear sounds, and sharks can sense electric currents that we can't. And to put in a kind word for our team, humans are born with hard-wired cognitive modules that make us sensitive to personal relationships in ways neither bees, dogs, elephants, or sharks can match. As we shall see, some of these modules make human leadership and followership possible.

The brains of all humans have about 10 billion neurons (brain cells) organized with more than 100 trillion potential connections. There are more possible connections in your brain at any one time than stars in the observable (pre-James Webb telescope) universe or grains of sand on Earth. The brain is only a three-pound piece of meat, but it is the most complex object in the known universe. You can do more things than the dung beetle because your brain is larger and has many more connections.

Our brains contain multi-thousands of hard-wired connections, each independent and hard-wired differently. For example, the wiring that enables you to sense danger is separate from the wiring that keeps you from having sex with your siblings, and activating one does not affect the other. These innate connections mean that the human mind is not a "blank slate" (Pinker 2002). Instead, we are born with ways of understanding and solving particular human problems.

Innate Human Behaviors

When human neurons are connected correctly, they lead to the most astoundingly complex processes, including those regulating human cultural and social phenomena (Tooby & Cosmides 1992). Our genes create hard-wired connections and specialized neurological circuits, designed through natural selection, that helped our ancestors survive (which is why you may be afraid of snakes even if you have never encountered one).

The human ability to both lead and follow is encoded in our genes, and the hard-wired connections for them are present at birth, even though they may not be expressed until later in life. Even though the human ability to lead and follow is genetic, there is no neurological 'center' for leadership and no 'leadership' gene. Despite the hype, there is no God gene, no gay gene, no intelligence gene, no language gene, and assuredly no leadership gene. Although all these behaviors have genetic components, no simple relationship exists between any single gene and complex human behavior.

The brains of humans everywhere share the same innate, evolved connections (Boyd & Silk 2003:498). Because of our shared genes and neural connections, all of us – including you as Chair and your departmental colleagues - are born with the potential to exhibit behaviors that make leadership and followership possible. Certain genes in specific human populations may create peripheral differences, such as eye or skin color, but these have no effects on brain functioning. Given similar environments and education when growing up, a kid from Nairobi is as likely to help create the first nuclear fission reactor as a kid from Nashville.

Our hard-wiring enables us to exhibit behaviors such as aggression, xenophobia, territoriality, sociality, reconciliation, autonomy, and dependence. They allow us to control others by establishing dominance hierarchies, displaying social emotions, recognizing in-group/out-group differences, forming coalitions, practicing reciprocity, recognizing individuals, empathizing with others, competing, and cooperating. We can purposefully mislead others, recognize deception, realize that others have minds similar to ours, and anticipate how others will react to a new situation by 'reading their minds.' We are born with the hard-wired ability to make judgments about social exchanges, live in groups, detect cheaters, manipulate the attention of others, and experience distress when deprived of human contact. We display emotions such as anger, happiness, sadness, fear, hesitancy, and apprehension (Savage-Rumbaugh & McDonald 1988). We can sense and respond to external threats, such as a cave bear in the Stone Age, or a malevolent dean or colleague today, by either fighting, fleeing, or freezing.

We are also born with the genetic imperative for kin altruism, meaning that we are hard-wired to give special attention to helping our relatives. We also practice reciprocal altruism, meaning that we trade favors and pay special attention to helping others who have helped us in the past. Kin and reciprocal altruism created millions of years ago still operate today as political or business leaders practice nepotism, benefit their relatives, or pardon friends who have previously helped them. We know the behaviors I have mentioned are enabled by genetics, not learning, because they exist today in chimpanzees.

Chimpanzee Leadership

Chimpanzees are our closest living relatives; they are our cousins and genetically more similar to humans than other ape species (Diamond 1992). Humans and chimps had a common ancestor six million years ago. After the two species separated, they remained approximately the same size for millions of years and had similar brains and mental capacities. The brain of a chimpanzee today is probably similar to the brain of our pre-human ancestors (Lawick-Goodall 1971). Humans and chimpanzees share 95 to 99 percent of their genes and have many of the same genetic and physiological features, so understanding chimpanzee leadership may help us understand our own.

All normal humans and chimps are born with or reliably grow brain connections that enable members of the two species to be dominant or submissive, depending on the environment and the others in the group. And both can instantly switch between these two types of behavior. When a chimp is in a group with others lower in rank, it rules the roost and is dominant. Put the same chimp in a group of higher-ranking animals, and it will instantly cower and become submissive. In the same way, you, as Chair, are likely to behave in a more dominant mode when you talk to a student and in a more submissive manner when you talk with your college's president. You and the chimp don't have to plan these changes in behavior purposefully – they happen naturally because of similarities in how their brains are hard-wired.

Chimps live in communities where animals are socially ranked and significantly influenced by the highest-ranking member, the alpha male (Chance & Jolly 1970). By all appearances, the alpha male is the group's 'leader.' Because his hair may stand on end, and his walk is exaggerated, he appears even larger than he is. Other chimps lower their bodies and greet him submissively, further increasing his appearance of unusual size (de Waal 1982). Observers identify the alpha as a leader because of his unique and vivid personality, confidence, and "extraordinariness" (Power 1991:165). But if he is deposed as the alpha by another chimp, his exaggerated size and self-confidence disappear; physical and behavioral characteristics quickly developed after being identified as a leader can just as quickly be lost when the leader is toppled.

The alpha chimp can't tell others what to do (because he can't talk), but he can dominate every other group member. The alpha has been called "demonic at unconscious and irrational levels" with a "temperamental goal…to intimidate the opposition, to beat them to a pulp, to erode their ability to challenge. Winning has become an end in itself" (Byrne & Peterson 1996:199). He can demand sexual favors, take food collected by others, punish them, and savor all the rewards the group offers. Rank is the focus of the alpha's life, and "his attempts to achieve and then maintain alpha status are cunning, persistent, energetic and time-consuming." The alpha male is the focus of everyone's attention. Submissive chimps watch him every minute to curry his favor or get out of his way. "The 'authority' of the top male chimpanzee has everything to do with a greedy, bullying style of domination" (Boehm 1999: 39). If this reminds you of any human boss you have experienced, you can blame it on genes we share with chimpanzees.

Pre-human males probably formed a rank system with higher-ranking males able to command respect from those lower in rank (Chance 1976; de Waal 2005). It is likely that, like chimpanzees, human males, bigger and stronger than females, commanded deference from others and reinforced their positions by physical force or by forming coalitions with other high-ranking males (Chance 1976). Some older females may be highly respected and chosen to act as 'arbiters' in disputes, where merely her focus on a conflict may be enough to end it; female chimps inherently want to restore peace (de Waal 1982). Under unusual circumstances, a female may become alpha.

Chimp displays of high status include hooting, swaying, rising on hind legs, and a charging run. "Full displays seem to be solely the province of adult males, and one consequence of displaying is that it directs the attention of others towards the displayer" (Reynolds & Luscombe 1976:112). As we shall see, one of your responsibilities as Chair is to direct your department's attention to important matters. In later chapters, I shall suggest ways to do this without hooting and making a charging run.

The aggressiveness and domination of males, seen in both chimpanzees and humans and made possible by similar genes, reflects the "indelible stamp of his lowly origins" to which Darwin referred. You can take the human out of the ape, but you can't take the ape out of the human.

Here come the Homo sapiens

The first anatomically correct humans appeared on Earth only 200,000 to 250,000 years ago, a mere blink of the evolutionary eye. We don't know how these early people enacted leadership. I like to think that even if they maintained ranking, early *Homo sapiens* were likelier to lead through autocratic benevolence than violence. However, unlike bones or stone tools studied by archeologists, leadership behavior leaves no evidence for us to ponder.

We can assume that these early humans probably communicated with each other with grunts, gestures, and facial expressions, as chimpanzees do today because they had no language. But humans developed sophisticated and symbolic language between 50,000 and 100,000 years ago for reasons still being debated. It almost appears that the cognitive modules that had led to the social dominance hierarchies of chimpanzees were replaced, in a relatively brief time, with different cognitive modules in humans, reflecting an egalitarian human nature. This dramatic change has been called The Great Leap Forward or The Cognitive Revolution. And a revolution it was! Once humans gained the ability to speak, the structure of the brain and the nature of leadership began to change. When complex language became possible, humans could exchange information about others' behavior and modify their thoughts (Boyd & Silk 2003). Genes still determined what was possible for us to do. But the neurological systems created by our genes often exist in pairs that appear to operate at cross-purposes. For example, we have one neural network permitting us to compete and another enabling us to cooperate. We are hard-wired to seek autonomy as well as dependence. We empathize with others but also torture and kill them. What determines which genetically-enabled path we follow?

Memes and Leadership

With the development of complex language, humans were now able to create 'soft wiring' in the brain through learning, in addition to hardwiring acquired at birth. As we learn, we make new connections between neurons and increase the strength and speed of these connections. Neuroscientists say that 'neurons that fire together, wire together,' so repeated firing of neurons due to a newly learned behavior means a new soft-wired neural network can be formed.

Once humans had evolved to use symbolic language, we were no longer controlled solely by our genes. Now we were also subject to the control of a second system of inheritance: cultural beliefs, values, and ideas, or 'memes,' that can be transmitted from one brain to another through language. Humans are the only species that have evolved a means of encoding and processing non-genetic information accumulated over time and transmitted through culture. And memes offered us new possibilities for enacting leadership and influencing others.

A Meme is More Than You Think it Is

A meme can glibly be thought of as 'an idea that catches on' or a 'virus of the mind that can affect the brain.' Thinking about it as a virus has a certain appeal since a meme, like a virus, is 'contagious'; one person 'catches it' and passes it on to another. Popular culture may solely consider memes as web-propagated pictures or symbols, but the full definition is more expansive. In his original formulation (1989:206), Dawkins said, "examples of memes are tunes, ideas, catch-phrases, clothes fashions, ways of making pots or building arches... Memes propagate themselves in the meme pool by leaping from brain to brain." And memes are the heritable building blocks of culture (Durham 1991).

Genes are transmitted vertically, from parents to children. Memes can also be transmitted vertically, but parents and kin are only one - and often not the most potent source - of memes. Memes are also communicated horizontally through the media, peer groups, speech, and the physical creations of people. Unlike genes, memes can be transmitted from younger to older and kin to non-kin. Genes and memes evolve, but memetic evolution can occur in real-time, while genetic change can take eons. Culture evolved because it can do things that genes alone can not and do them more rapidly (Richerson & Boyd 2004).

Memes are the components of our learned skills, beliefs, artifacts, and behavioral traditions. Just as genes are biological recipes, memes are cultural recipes. Children of Muslims are likely to be Muslim; children of academics are likely to go to college. As Gilbert and Sullivan observed in *Iolanthe*, "every boy and every gal/that's born into the world alive/is either a little Liberal/or else a little Conservative!" What we are taught as young children around the metaphorical kitchen table, or in the madrasa, the Quaker meeting hall, or the campus, become memes and persistent patterns of thought that, once learned, are resistant to change.

Humans, of course, retain the hard-wiring bequeathed to us by our non-human and early-human ancestors. But now, in addition to neural connections dictated by the vertical heredity of genes, we also are influenced by vertical and horizontal neural connections created by socially-created memes. Language changed the nature of leadership. The genetic rule 'be good to people who share your genes' evolved after the development of speech into the human memetic rule 'be good to people who share your memes.' "Memes are part of human cumulative cultural evolution" (Richerson & Boyd 2004:107). It may take a village to raise a child, but it takes replicating memes and cumulative cultural evolution to make a village - or an academic department.

Hardware and Software

If the networks of neurons in the brain created by genes can be thought of as the hardware that permits us to act and think, memes, by analogy, can be thought of as the cultural software or programs our brains 'run' (Durham 1991). I mentioned earlier that genes allow humans to display dominance or submission. Memes allow humans to identify the circumstances under which each behavior is appropriate. We inherit this soft-wired cultural software from the people around us, and we pass it on to others as we communicate with them (Balkin 1998).

Repetition - hearing certain words, seeing different images, or observing others behaving in different ways - soft-wires some brain connections and strengthens them. A person who has internalized the memes 'an eye for an eye' and 'kill the infidels' is likely to behave quite differently and have a brain that physically is wired differently than a person who has internalized the memes 'turn the other cheek' and 'love they neighbor.' The meaning of leadership in a culture that has accepted democracy is significantly different from the definition in a culture satisfied with an autocracy. Faculty think differently in a college where decisions come from the top down than one in which the norm of shared authority has been embraced.

Genes vs. Memes

Our genes determine human universals (Brown 1991), demonstrating how we are alike. But how genes are expressed may depend on memes created by social learning that explain the cultural differences we see around us. The continuing tensions between genes and memes, between the constant and the divergent, are revealed in the uniquely human ability to override genes with memes and contribute to leadership's central complexities.

Can memes overrule genes? It's so common we usually don't even think about it, but instances abound. For example, humans (like all animals) have the genetic imperative to pass our genes on to future generations. But not all humans behave that way. What compels a couple to adopt an unrelated child? Why does a priest remain celibate? Why does a marine fall on top of a live grenade? Why do firefighters rush into a burning building? These behaviors all prevent the transmission of genes. The memes these people have inherited prove to be even stronger.

A significant task of a leader is to create social order. Leaders can create social order in two ways. One is establishing social ranks and maintaining them using coercion and violence as chimpanzees (and perhaps our pre-human ancestors) did. But, as we have seen, coercive power in human groups leads to alienation. The other way to establish order is not based on our genetic predisposition towards coercion but on our memetic ability to enact the opposing genetically-based tendencies for empathy and cooperation. Cooperation returns more benefits than competition, and we cooperate because it is in our best interests to do so (Axelrod 1984). Coercive force can influence what people do, but the appeal to their common memes often is even more powerful. Memes like "one for all, all for one," "follow me," or "leave no one behind" can lead people to heroic behaviors that override their genetic interest in self-preservation.

Gene-enabled development of empathy has given all humans "the prerequisites for morality: a tendency to develop social norms and enforce them, the capacity for sympathy, mutual aid and a sense of fairness, and mechanisms for conflict resolution" (de Waal 1996:39). But whether and how these are used depends on memes. Our genes have also made the development of moral altruism possible, represented by the words "do unto others as you would have them do unto you." This Golden Rule is derived from the basic principles of exchange reciprocity and reciprocal altruism. These evolved in our Paleolithic ancestors as some of our primary moral sentiments (Shermer 2004). While humans may instinctively know it is wrong to hurt another human being, memes created through local usage may determine whether they define you as being 'one of us' or 'one of the other." If they see you as 'one of us,' you're in luck. If they see you as 'other,' you are potentially in jeopardy, and modern humans have reserved their most barbaric behavior for those outside the group.

The brain connections created by our genes make language possible, but the vocabulary is a meme-related tradition created by learning and social transmission and is arbitrary. Genes and memes work together. That's why your children can speak (genes) grammatically correct English (memes) effortlessly, while Tanaka-san's child speaks fluent Japanese. They share the same hard-wired genetic modules that make language possible but have different soft-wired memes that make their speech distinctive and their cultures different.

Memes and Norms

Widely shared memes develop into norms, and following norms leads not to biological fitness but social and cultural fitness. What kinds of memes are most likely to be adopted and passed on? The most successful memes are "altruistic, cooperative, and generous ways of behaving...If people are altruistic, they become popular, and because they are popular, they are copied, and because they are copied, their memes spread more widely than the memes of not-so-altruistic people" (Blackmore 1999:154). Memetic evolution always builds on what was already there. A meme can change over time, but the older memes are still remembered (there are people called Historians, whose job is to ensure they are not forgotten even if they are no longer in use).

Fortunately, while all of us have genes for selfishness, most academics today override them with gene-enabled memes that lead us instead to base our behavior on justice, fairness, and compassion. Humans appear to be hard-wired (from birth) and soft-wired (through the social interactions that can alter the brain's architecture) to behave reciprocally. As long as reciprocally-minded group members are in the majority, a group will likely move its moral arc towards cooperative behavior. The rise of the meme did not end humans' genetic evolution, but it made our continued genetic change of secondary importance. Genes will still modestly influence future human development, but memes will write human history.

As Chair, you are in a critical position to create and spread positive memes that seek to satisfy higher needs, engage your follower's whole person and raise everyone to higher levels of motivation and morality (Burns 1978). You can use memes to create attractive new visions of the department's future and engage in higher performance levels. You can't do anything as a Chair to affect your colleagues' genes. But you can do a lot to influence the department's culture and the memes that 'infect' their brains to help them 'decide' which one potential outcome of conflicting genes will be enacted. One of your roles as Chair is to ensure the best memes win!

Chapter Five

Leadership Evolves in the Gardens of Eden

As a Chair, you are responsible for the performance and well-being of a small group. You know that genes make alternative behaviors possible, while memes will likely determine which behaviors are enacted. Theories about small groups and analyses of leadership in the previous chapters provide some perspectives about actions you might consider to improve your department and make your term as Chair more successful. Twentieth and 21st Century scholars and practitioners developed these ideas about human groups and leadership. Do they reflect human universals, or are they dependent on specific times and cultures? This question is difficult to answer by looking only at contemporary groups operating in complex civilizations.

Perhaps we can gain some insight by looking at the past. Small human groups have existed for tens of thousands – perhaps hundreds of thousands– of years. Humans have always lived in groups, as did the primate species that preceded us (Carporael et al. 2005). Some ancient group practices may inform our view of how contemporary small groups can become more effective.

Let's go back – way back – to the Stone Age to see how small human groups functioned 20,000 years ago. Humans then lived in an environment that did not include any of the institutions we take for granted today. There were no kings to establish social hierarchies, no institutions to identify those who could give orders, and no laws to codify desirable behavior. None of our contemporary technologies or materials existed. Whatever was produced was made of stone or other naturally occurring materials. What was leadership like among humans living in this primal environment? Did they do anything that can help us understand small group leadership today?

The Stone Age

The Stone Age lasted over a million years until the last ice age ended approximately 12,000 years ago. Some of what we know about the way of life then comes from the work of archaeologists who study ancient sites and artifacts to shed light on how our ancestors looked, behaved, and thought (Mithen 1996). Other evidence comes from 20th-century anthropologists who studied bands of isolated people living in remote parts of the world, presumably much as our Stone Age ancestors did (Cashdan 1989).

Our ancestors of 20,000 years ago were generally civilized folks, at least when dealing with members of their own band or with nearby bands with whom cordial relationships had been established. Their brains were almost identical to ours. While some human bands still lived in openings carved out of caves, many lived in rough houses built out of branches, mud, stones, bones, and animal hides. These homes were often set in a circle, with a large communal fire pit at the center around which the group might gather. Our ancestors lived in groups of associated families that might have included as few as 20 to as many as 150 people (we'll see in the next chapter why 150 people could operate as a 'small group' then, but not now).

Some bands established semi-permanent winter and summer camps, while others moved their camps every few days. Bands could remain together year-round or separate into smaller family groups when resources were seasonally tight. They could then come together to socialize, trade, and hold ceremonies when resources became abundant (Cashden 1989). The beginnings of agriculture and the domestication of flocks or herds of animals were still 10,000 years in the future.

Our ancestors universally were 'foragers' or 'hunter-gatherers.' This social structure of a group of a few associated bands of related nuclear families was almost uniformly found in foraging societies all over the Earth. It existed in all habitats and has been called "almost an inevitable kind of organization" (Service 1971:97). Group living, as humans found out, had many benefits. We are a 'contact species' and derive pleasure and a sense of security from being together (Larson 1976).

These groups had characteristics that still overtly or latently persist in some groups today. They had a shared psychological reality and a shared sense of identity. They distinguished between in-groups and out-groups and were wary of out-group members. The in-group was clearly and positively identified as good, "hence the self is imbued with positive value" (Hollinshead et al. 2005:107). Group members reacted strongly to those who did not conform to the group. Loyalty was to the group rather than to individuals, and members were willing to sacrifice their self-interest for the group's welfare.

Families were the basic units of social groups. Males (primarily but not exclusively) hunted, and women (mainly but not exclusively) gathered plants, seeds, and fruit. Men dominated political life, with "women and children expected to be submissive" (Wade 2006:65). When women came of age, they often left their bands to find partners in other bands. These inter-band marriages made it possible for people to visit non-band relatives if they were in need. 'Visiting the in-laws' (and perhaps even mother-in-law jokes?) may be a tens-of-thousands of years old human tradition.

Universal People

While many anthropologists study the differences between people, others examine their similarities, leading to extensive descriptions of what has been called the Universal People (UP). UP is a composite of the common characteristics found in all known cultures (Brown 1991) that must also have existed in these prehistoric bands. An incomplete listing of universals includes over 400 traits (Pinker 2002). Examples include inheritance, status, having false beliefs, dancing, using fire, division of labor by sex, gossip, sexual modesty, mother-son incest taboo, using metaphors, marriage, reciprocity, the male preference for younger women, intragroup conflict, a sense of 'fairness,' body adornment, and wariness around snakes (sorry to mention snakes again, but if your prehistoric ancestor wasn't careful around them, you might not be reading this today). These common characteristics were genetically based and had a biological explanation, but how they were enacted was cultural and was created and supported by memes. For example, while the concept of inheritance existed in all bands, whether it followed patrilinear, matrilinear, or other rules differed among groups.

The universal way of life 20,000 years ago existed in what I call the Gardens of Eden. The ice-age environment was difficult for groups living in colder climates or higher altitudes in northern Europe and North America but not for those living in temperate parts of Africa, Australia, and South America. Whether in the desert, jungle, forest edge, or open prairie, the Gardens were characterized by abundant animals to hunt, adequate food, close and supportive relationships, and ample time for leisure. Some researchers have referred to these groups as "the original affluent society" because "subsistence work [was] intermittent, leisure time [was] abundant, and nutrition status [was] excellent" (Cashdan 1989:22-23). As told in the Old Testament and the Quran, the story of Adam and Eve may reflect a meme deeply embedded in our minds of an earlier era in which many humans lived in a comfortable and resource-rich environment. Genesis 3:17 tells us that only after humans slouched out of the Gardens were we condemned to eat our bread by the sweat of our brows until we died. This prediction came true with the invention of agriculture, but that was still 10,000 years in the future.

Life in the Gardens of Eden

In the Gardens, genes, memes, and the changing environment led to new ideas about how humans should live together.

Egalitarianism. Millions of years ago, our pre-human ancestors probably enacted hard-wired cognitive systems emphasizing strength and physical aggression. Their genetic imperatives directed much of their violent behavior; they did what their genes required because they had no choice. The alpha male ruled over a hierarchy. But the keyword to describe bands of our hunter-gatherer human ancestors 20,000 years ago was not 'hierarchical' but 'egalitarian' (Weissner 1996).

It is impossible to know precisely when egalitarian societies began. Early humans couldn't form one because, at a minimum, egalitarianism requires language to influence the intentions of others, permit the sharing of values, and enact delayed reciprocity. Egalitarianism had to wait until humans could deal with symbolic thought, perhaps 50,000 to 100,000 years ago. Regardless of when it started, it is clear that humans in the Gardens of Eden lived in an egalitarian social order.

Groups of 20 to 100 people, or perhaps slightly more, worked together in the Gardens to achieve common goals. These communities were self-sufficient, self-regulating residential groups with no formal leaders or political hierarchies and responsive to no higher political authority. Human foragers in bands are always egalitarian, with no classes, no differences in rank, and weak leadership (Boehm 1997). Still, in the absence of formal structure, "group activities unfold, plans are made, and decisions are arrived at - all apparently without a clear focus of authority or influence" (Lee 1979:343). Group members in the Gardens didn't aspire to leadership or compete for it. No one had authority over anyone else, and decisions were made by consensus (Knauft 1991).

There were two exceptions to egalitarianism; both grew out of family statuses and may still influence many groups today. Personal inequalities existed based on both age and sex (Service 1971). The words of older people carried greater weight in discussions (Lee 1979), and the voices of youth were ignored. Men were usually older than the women they married (fewer women lived as long as men due to childbirth risks), so men had an advantage based on seniority and learned experience. In addition, men were bigger and stronger than women, suggesting male dominance. However, unlike chimpanzees, there was no alpha male in egalitarian communities, and the influence of leadership was subtle and indirect. Leadership as influence was no longer the privilege of the few at the top of a hierarchy but was shared by (almost) all. For many groups, 'all' meant 'men' as the heads of families. The extent of female participation in the decision-making of these bands probably varied among groups. In most groups, men were the politically active members of the band. In others, women may have had an equal voice (Lee 1979).

Social Regulation. Every functional and self-sustaining social system must be regulated in some fashion if there is to be order. Social regulation in the Gardens of Eden occurred through people's intimate, regular, face-to-face interactions. Continued group membership was the most critical aspect of their existence. Everyone knew the group's mutual behavioral expectations and its members' temperaments. Norms were reinforced by sharing, providing companionship and protection, and responding positively to those who behaved consistently with them. Deviants would draw sarcasm and a loss of regard by others. Everyone knew that punishment approved by the group would damage an individual's reputation, and a good reputation was necessary to gain the benefits of reciprocal altruism (Lee 1979).

In an egalitarian group, physical dominance was not practical. In its place arose a complex set of social skills, such as making trustworthy commitments and following a strategy of fair play. These skills required identifying with other group members, appreciating equality, and committing to share. Group members helped others, being confident that others would help them.

Egalitarianism was reinforced by social norms that discouraged arrogance and encouraged humility and understatement. Groups, then and now, could tolerate individual differences, but not those whose behavior violated group norms (Hollingshead et al. 2005). Anthropologists found that in one 20th-century band, a hunter never boasts of a kill. Instead, he apologizes to the band for bringing back such a small and worthless animal. One band member said, "we refuse one who boasts, for someday his pride will make him kill somebody. So we always speak of his meat as worthless… In this way we cool his heart and make him gentle" (Lee 1979:246). This band also diminished pride through the practice of trading arrows among the men. The meat from the hunt did not belong to the man who killed the animal but to the man who originally owned the arrow. The owner of the arrow gained prestige and the right to distribute the meat to the group.

Norms, then and now, were considered by group members as 'the ways things should be done.' Norms developed as conformity to certain behaviors were rewarded or punished by the group. Rewards could take the form of "acceptance and approval, signaled through seeking out, respect, deference, friendship, affectionate behavior, and the like" (Power 1991:182). Leaders had a stake in preserving norms and, therefore, a responsibility to help enforce them. While leaders could not create norms, leaders emerged because of the cultural norms about leadership (Gibb 1969:205). Compliance with norms is essential in egalitarian groups, which offer the compelling, intangible rewards of belonging. Norms led to a "behavioral public good" that everyone enforced even at some cost to themselves (Fehr & Gachter 2000:166).

This social dynamic of egalitarianism had several advantages over earlier systems based on social dominance. Dominance systems require significant energy expenditure by both the dominant and subordinate individuals who must continuously keep track of and respond to social order challenges. In egalitarian societies, order is maintained through memes and internalized norms, thus lowering the level of arousal of all participants. Egalitarian systems in which all had a voice made it possible to tap into the collective memories of dozens of individuals whose experiences might not be expressed in a more hierarchical society. This provided a rich source of information and knowledge of frequently occurring events (Mithen 1990).

Humans abided by group rules (Dunbar 1999), particularly when internalized, self-developed, and coupled with a graduated level of group punishment. The social norm of cooperation was accompanied by the norms of autonomy and individual self-direction. These norms may have appeared opposed to each other but were complementary. Individuals lived their lives as they wished but within prescribed group roles. Individuals were free to "make their own choices: to take part or not to take part in any activity, to choose whether or not to be organized by others and by which others, to join or not to join, to come or to go. These choices led to a high level of 'independent conformity' - not to be confused with obedience (behavior regulated by a higher authority)" (Power 1995:672).

Egalitarianism was reinforced by memes leading to social norms that decreased the importance of leadership.

Groups had an ethos of sharing "that selectively extends to the entire group the cooperation and altruism found within the family" (Boehm 1999: 67). Genes provided the basis for using the family to define 'us': memes allowed extending the definition of 'us' to perhaps include a small number of nearby groups with whom they had established trading or interfamily relationships.

All groups in human foraging societies followed the rule that all meat must be shared equally among the different families (Wrangham 2001). The band was a unit of sharing, and if sharing broke down, the band would cease to exist. "This principle of reciprocity within the band has been reported for hunter-gatherers on every continent and in every kind of environment" (Lee 1979:118). It would certainly have existed in the Gardens. Expectations of sharing food help stabilize a band; band members gave to others because they knew that others would give to them when needed.

Leadership and Influence. Instead of having formal and permanent leaders, communities in the Gardens of Eden coordinated their activities through temporary, informal leaders (Gibb 1969). Individuals with qualities beneficial to the group, such as "knowledge, ritual expertise, abilities in planning and organization, mediation, hunting skill, generosity, defense, and interaction with outsiders" (Weissner 1996:174), were accorded prestige. The most prestigious may have had the most influence, but only when discussing matters within their areas of competence. Leaders in the Gardens persuaded rather than decided. No one sought the leadership role, and leaders changed as the specific problems did. The group conferred leadership, and leadership was never seized by a member (Power 1991).

The earlier pre-human genetic predisposition to dominate, if possible, had not been eradicated. It still existed but was countered by memes that reflected the desire and commitment to resist domination and accept an equal relationship as a good outcome. Even though an individual might take the initiative in a situation, everyone was prepared to listen to alternatives, to change their mind, and to agree to accept influence from another who had greater knowledge (Erdal & Whiten 1996).

The band permitted and expected specific members to exert unusual influence under particular circumstances; in exchange, these members were expected to cede influence to others when circumstances changed. Through the development of norms of reciprocity, humans in small groups could behave cooperatively without the need for formal structure (Ostrom 2000). Cooperation was likely to occur automatically in small hunter-gatherer groups because everyone's activities were monitored by everyone else.

Leadership emerged in response to members' felt need to turn to an individual who could help the group solve a particular problem at a specific time. During this problem-solving process, group members who helped initiate or control others' behavior fulfilled leadership roles. The group could concurrently confer high status on many qualified people (Boehm 1999:38). Consequently, groups may have had many leaders at different times and even several simultaneously (Gibb 1969). Leadership, or non-coercive influence, was exercised at any particular moment by that individual on whom the group's attention was focused.

Leadership in these groups depended more on the density of potential leaders than any specific person's presence. Fortunately, leadership in the Gardens was both dense and dispersed; almost anyone could be a leader at one time or another if they were seen as having the requisite expertise. A group of our Stone Age ancestors would almost certainly be better off if its members paid attention to an expert tracker, a proficient healer, an excellent storyteller, or a superior weapons maker as the occasion demanded, rather than rely on the wisdom of a single person regardless of their brilliance.

Since the group itself was unstructured, leadership without authority was based on "personal attributes, personality, skills, knowledge, wisdom... It [was] temporary and shifting according to circumstantial needs" (Power 1991:47). The suggestions of someone acknowledged as a successful hunter would be given unusual weight when hunting strategies were formed. An acknowledged warrior would command their attention and lead if neighboring groups intruded into the camp's territory. A person with a good memory for myths would be influential when discussing rituals. "Thus, a great many normally charismatic individuals of both sexes [were] influential (temporary leaders) when some special skill they possess [was] needed" (Power 1995:673).

Influence was thus likely to be exerted by people who were seen as competent in the task being discussed and understood to share the group's norms and values (Hollander 1969). There was no mechanism to assure compliance, and, even after consensus was reached, those who disagreed were free to go their own way if they wished.

Our ancestors valued the ability to exercise non-coercive influence because they realized that survival was difficult without the coordination and consensus that influentials could provide (de Waal 1996). When the group had an internal disagreement that needed to be fairly resolved, influence by specific individuals could be solicited and eagerly supported by followers. In such cases, this willingness to voluntarily cede to another a limited amount of their autonomy may have been due to the unconscious operation of a cognitive cost/benefit analysis. The chances of becoming alpha in a group might be, for example, one in 15. That means that the chances of being dominated would be 14 in 15. The trade-off for not being able to dominate others is to be sure that you will not be dominated (Boehm 1997). Put another way and crediting genetic and memetic imperatives, "all men seek to rule but if they cannot rule they prefer to be equal" (Schneider 1979:210). Memes overwhelm genes again!

Leadership in the Gardens had to be considered by the followers to be legitimate to be effective. Legitimacy was related to the follower's perception of the leader and how that leader came to power (Hollander 1978:45). Leadership in small foraging groups was legitimate when it flowed from followers' recognition of others' expertise or experience, the belief that group members retained their independence of action, and an understanding that leaders in one realm will not attempt to control the behavior of others (Power 1995).

Sometimes there were specific circumstances, such as when the group had an internal disagreement that needed to be fairly resolved, in which a respected elder could become a temporary leader. Older members could act as peacekeepers and settlers of disputes (Power 1991). But after immediate crises were resolved, individuals who tried to extend their influence into a perpetual status were put back in their place. They remained respected citizens without special status (Erdal & Whiten 1996). Our ancestors considered leaders as "disposable, desertable, and generally dispensable" (Boehm 2000:79).

Decision-Making. Our ancestors did not accept the authority of anyone; they listened, and then the group decided. Everyone was always watching to protect themselves from leaders who might seek more permanent power. If a talk with elders didn't have the required result, deviants could be shunned and killed as a last resort. A member of the deviant's family often did the deed to prevent inter-family vendettas.

There were no social classes or ranks among hunter-gatherers; decision-making was decentralized and by consensus (Boehm 1997). For these small human groups, managing conflict was a significant concern. Their ability to use language increased the possibilities for cooperation, mutual assistance, resolving disputes, and arriving at solutions seen as fair by the group members. As one anthropologist put it, referring to 20th-century hunter-gatherers (Boyd & Silk 2003:424-5), "conflicts within the group [we]re resolved by talking and talking, sometimes half or all of the night, for nights and weeks on end." And so, we have discovered the roots of faculty meetings today.

Discussions around the council fire were informal, and everyone in the group could speak if they wished. Those believed to have specific and appropriate skills were paid the most attention as they moved towards consensus. Influence was less a reflection of how a person was seen as talking and more related to the degree to which others were "listening with respect" to that person (Erdal & Whiten 1996:145). Dynamic, emergent, and dispersed leadership was not monolithic but divided and not predicated on conflict, competition, or submission. "Again and again, leadership in small groups proved to be keyed to integrity rather than imposed or inherited authority" (Shepard & Shepard 1998:156). Individuals could willingly accept a somewhat different consensus from their own view because a lack of consensus might mean the group might not sustain itself. If a group's existence was challenged, the benefits of shared resources, protection, and sociality might be lost.

The temporary leader's role was not to make a final decision but to help the group reach a consensus. Group members around the central council fire moved between leadership and followership roles; both were valued. Individuals retained their autonomy because they did not rely on accepted authority but ultimately decided whether to follow the group's consensus. Followers were "active, rather than passive, group members, and ... group and leader functions depend heavily on them" (Power 1991:171). Although effective individuals were recognized and generally heeded, the function of leadership "remain[ed] situational, and [was] not transformed into a permanent social role with a distinct status" (Erdal & Whiten 1994:177).

Expertise. Becoming influential in a hunter-gatherer community required developing a reputation for expertise in some area of concern to the group. Younger people had difficulty being accepted as influential by their elders because developing expertise takes time and experience that younger people could not offer. A stone-age storyteller had to hear and remember many stories, and a tool-maker had to master an intricate craft. A hunter could improve his skills to track and predict where animals could be located. Older hunters not only knew more than younger ones, but they also were better able to assess the relevance of the things they knew to the task at hand. Older people recognized patterns and evaluated situations similar to those they had experienced. Perhaps this experience is the basis for 'wisdom.'

Experts develop richer schemas than non-experts, and they can encode and retrieve pertinent information faster (Brown et al. 2004). Experts can draw on experience and intuition to make decisions quickly and accurately (Gladwell 2005:107). This ability to be 'right,' albeit with limited information, may be a hallmark of those accepted as human leaders. Prehistoric bands appeared tacitly aware of the modern rule that it takes at least 10,000 hours of concentrated effort to become an expert in any field.

Leveling. The human unwillingness to be unfairly subjected to another's power was institutionalized through several processes of 'leveling' in the Gardens. Leveling involves behaviors by collectively assertive followers that reduce dominance by removing individuals from the group's focus of attention. The genetic forces that fostered cooperation were strengthened by memetic group norms that disciplined those who refused to cooperate. Hunter-gatherer groups used several leveling processes to inhibit individuals from being overly aggressive or attempting to give orders to others. Social sanctions began with criticism of their behavior, which could be reinforced by ridicule. Attempts to give orders to others were countered by disobedience or ostracism. If all else failed, assassination could be the ultimate sanction (Boehm 1993).

Sharing and Cooperation. A limited degree of sharing had been part of the pre-human and human repertoire for millions of years, but sharing in the Gardens went well beyond what could be explained simply as a property of kin altruism or reciprocity. Human groups exhibited "a cluster of features which appear to act as the functional core of the societies" (Erdal & Whiten 1996:140). Humans with genes that favored cooperation would have been more successful than others in attracting mates and reproducing. 'Niceness' can be genetically transmitted in a social order in which aggressive deviants are ostracized.

People shared because "an extraordinarily wide range of risks must be pooled over the long term through reciprocal relationships that have very special conditions." The conditions were that those with food, goods, or valuables must give to those in need without stipulating that they must be specifically reciprocated later. Instead, reciprocation was expected to be balanced over a lifetime, thus enacting delayed reciprocity. "Those who have things of value but do not give [we]re subject to social control through gossip, ridicule, or ostracism" (Weissner 1996:186).

Sharing and cooperation had genetic antecedents that were shaped by mimetic understandings. The genetic precursors led humans first to kin altruism (help those who share your genes), then to reciprocal altruism (help those who have helped you), and finally to indirect altruism. Indirect altruism occurs when someone acts generously to an unknown person with signs (same language, country, religion, club, hobby, alma mater, etc.) signaling probable cooperation. Anyone traveling overseas and providing or receiving aid to or from a compatriot has experienced it.

The Vigilant Moral Community

Hunter-gatherers lived in small, coherent groups, thus making possible the development of a vigilant moral community - "a strongly latent coalition of the entire group, which actively unites to deal with deviants" (Boehm 1997:353). Members of a moral community have a shared understanding of how people should treat each other and what kind of behavior is right or wrong. The moral community based on reciprocity is self-policing; cooperation is reinforced, and assertiveness is punished (Axelrod 1984). Leaders in a moral community do not give orders or make demands on others (Lee 1979). If anyone tries to issue an order, no one will obey it.

People in the Gardens tended to think alike. They shared the same genes, and their brains contained many of the same memes. This made members of a band both genetic and memetic 'kin.' Everyone was in regular communication with everyone else, so ideas, once expressed, were either socially reinforced or extinguished by the responses of the vigilant community. Gossiping provided "an information network that [enabled] an entire group to respond to transgressions on a well-informed and collective basis... Specific and detailed communication [was] highly pertinent to building a moral consensus " (Boehm 2000:187). Individual autonomy operating within the context of required social behaviors meant that egalitarianism was continuously reinforced in the moral community.

A moral community is based on maintaining social relationships within the group, understanding what behaviors are acceptable under specified conditions, and the group's ability to correct and ultimately sanction those whose conduct is unacceptable. Members of a moral community contribute what they can and take what they need from a common resource base. There is no need for a strict or immediate balancing of value given and taken. But free-riders are identified and sanctioned to bring them back into line.

In general, everyone in the moral community is believed to be good; this, in turn, may have led to perceptions that those outside it were uniformly bad or wrong. At worst, it may have led those in the moral group to see those outside it as non-people, thus justifying treating them inhumanely and without compassion. The agreed-on values of any specific moral community arise from culture, and different communities may have quite different views of what behaviors are or are not acceptable. However, since the potential for egalitarianism was universal among hunter-gatherers, its potential must have been genetically grounded (Erdal & Whiten 1994).

Memes

Because they had language and norms, we are sure that our ancestors also had memes, although we cannot know what their memes were. Perhaps their memes were related to respect for expertise, sharing food, accepting the dominance of older men, equality (at least among men), and assenting to leadership from those who were generous, fair, and self-effacing. Remember that the design of an arrowhead, the structure of a home, or the preferred shape of a firepit were all memes. They were conceived by minds in the past, transmitted to others as part of their group's cumulative culture, and realized in stone or wood. More social memes such as a fear of strangers, the obligation to share, and the identification of which plants were edible must have been passed along through language from parents to their children, reinforced by others in the band, and eventually codified and passed on to later generations.

Bands living in different environments, such as by a river, near a seashore, or on a mountain, probably trafficked in memes concerning the attributes, dangers, and particular challenges of where they lived. In all situations, the ability to use complex language to tell others what was permitted or forbidden and offer simple examples that could be internalized was made possible both by nature and nurture. With memes, members of bands could now teach others the use of technologies that enriched and protected them and ensure a community of comity and peace in ways that were not available to our earlier pre-human ancestors.

As Darwin said, humans still bear the indelible stamp of their lowly origin. That was as true 20,000 years ago as it is today. But once we could use language and create memes as the building blocks of culture, some of that indelible stamp could be redirected or overcome in ways that made us more human.

Are any norms and memes that made life comfortable, sustainable, and moral 20,000 years ago applicable in today's colleges? Is there any value in trying to become an exemplary Chair by emulating leadership in the Stone-Age?

Chapter Six

How to be an Exemplary Department Chair

Human beings will be happier - not when they cure cancer or get to Mars or eliminate racial prejudice or flush Lake Erie but when they find ways to inhabit primitive communities again. – Kurt Vonnegut Jr., *Wampeters, Foma and Granfalloons.*

Our societies probably work best if they mimic as closely as possible the small-scale communities of our ancestors. (deWaal 2005:233*)*

Thomas Merton says man went wrong when he left the Stone Age- -Wendell Berry, as cited by Dorothy Wickenden, Late Harvest."

Informal and temporary leadership enabled rather than directed people in the long-ago past. But the Gardens of Eden, with its small, isolated bands, and Stone-Age technology, are increasingly remote. Is what was possible then in small, self-governing groups still achievable in our global, competitive, hierarchical, interconnected, ends-oriented, and often amoral world?

It may be more difficult, but you can try. You, your department colleagues, and college administrators share the same genes and many of the same memes related to higher education. Your department members have gone through similar studies, were educated in graduate schools in the same discipline, belong to the same small departmental group, have selected you as its leader (I hope), and believe in the value of education. Like their Stone-Age ancestors, they value expertise, expect independence of action, and question authority. They are likely to support cooperative norms as long as norms of autonomy and self-direction accompany them. In addition to memes widely shared throughout the college's faculty and administration, your disciplinary colleagues share many unique memes from their past training and experience. You are unlikely to succeed as Chair if you do not know these memes.

What can you do with your knowledge of the dual heritage of genes and memes that perhaps you might not have thought about before? Should you try to become a present-day Stone-Age Chair? Many of the suggestions presented earlier in the sections titled Management Made (Relatively) Simple in Chapter Two and Leadership Made (Relatively) Simple in Chapter Three are consistent with this objective. But now, after considering how life was lived 20,000 years ago, let's be more specific. I think you can become a better Chair not by reading the latest books on leadership but by considering some of our Stone-Age ancestors' gene- and meme-enabled leadership practices. You can modify these ancient practices to suit the norms and structures of your department and college. Here are some suggestions drawn from our past.

Distribute Leadership

Our ancestors of 20,000 years ago did not accept the authority of a permanent leader. Perhaps an elder might be persuaded to mediate a disagreement. Still, this person performed only a ministerial function and was easily replaced. Instead of a permanent leader, members of the stone-age band influenced each other based on perceived expertise.

Our ancestors' business consisted of debating questions of survival: What kind of animal shall we hunt tomorrow? When should we plan to move to our Winter quarters? How can we overcome this sickness that has affected many of us? Every group member could speak to these questions. Still, most attention was paid to those believed to have particular expertise: the most successful hunter, the oldest member with memories of past seasonal treks, or the shaman whose magic resolved past illnesses. How can we recreate this shared leadership system based on experience and expertise today?

One way to encourage leadership among your department members is by making them specialists and experts on matters of significant department consequence. As Chair, you have a multitude of management responsibilities. You can give lip service to all of them but usually cannot provide extended attention to each one. If you agree to share the burden of these tasks with departmental colleagues, you can help groom their leadership qualities and free your time to pursue other non-routine department objectives. You would be able to 'share arrows' as our ancestors did so that your followers receive recognition even for a project you initiated.

As an example, one department member could be responsible for enrollment data. This person could make a formal report to the department each year detailing the number of students in courses, the number of majors, enrollment by year, enrollment by age, sex, and ethnicity, enrollment trends over time, attrition rates, graduation rates, and related matters. This person could serve as the 'expert' and chair the discussion whenever enrollment issues were on the department meeting's agenda. Other department members could fill similar roles when discussing technology, innovations in the discipline, distance learning, or diversity.

Here is another example. Faculty in many departments are only vaguely aware, through gossip, of colleagues' teaching, research, and service activities. A faculty 'expert' could create a Faculty Work Activity Dashboard (O' Meara, Beise, Culpepper, Musra & Jaeger 2020), displaying annual data to show faculty work activity. The expert could lead a department discussion about the comparative dashboard data to determine whether any differences seen were just or unjust, fair or unfair. By "making the invisible visible" (p. 38), the dashboard could show inequities in workload. Instead of relying solely on workload gossip, the dashboard could help relieve the discomfort that often results when determining if everyone is doing their share. Because the dashboard offers transparency, it can also lead to accountability in which the entire department participates in establishing group norms. If that happens, you, as a Chair, can act as a discussion leader rather than an enforcer.

If your institution permits it, you can give these department 'experts' titles such as Assistant Chair for Enrollment to give them some charisma of office and something to put on their CV. Faculty appointed or elected for these roles would be the person on whom department members focus attention, rather than on you, when their reports or areas of expertise are included on the department's meeting agenda.

Establishing diverse nodes of expertise in the department has specific consequences that may not initially be obvious. Remember that leadership density in a foraging group is more important than one person's leadership. The same principle holds for an academic department. Having specialists increases department members' awareness without requiring them to study these issues individually and deeply.

As always, enact such new ideas slowly. Start with just one 'assistant chair'. If the department accepts the idea, wait at least a semester before trying to establish another.

Increase Interaction and Sociality

Your department is a small, coherent group functioning as part of a larger and more complex organization whose size and intricate structure make interaction, cooperation, and friendship increasingly tricky. Our genes make it probable that we will cooperate in small groups. But as groups become larger, opportunities for continuous interaction decrease. One of your leadership roles as Chair is to increase regular and frequent interaction among department members to reinforce the cooperative systems built into human nature. Remember, our genes permit us to cooperate – but they also allow us to compete. When people in a small group interact regularly, they are more likely to share their memes and to see other members as part of the group.

Belonging to a small group is a primary human genetic need from our pre-human ancestors to the present. Belonging increases cooperation among group members. People find comfort in belonging and fear danger and uncertainty without it. The need for belonging to a group is so great for modern humans that being banished from a community and forbidden to maintain social relationships with its members can be more painful than death. One significant role of a Chair is to engender and maintain feelings of belonging among members, accepting and protecting even deviants and 'the least among us' as our ancestors did.

You can promote forums for interaction and design them to be continuing, frequent, and durable. The relatively small size of an academic department makes this possible but not inevitable. The group members "must be able to build direct, personal relationships. To allow the free flow of information, they have to interact casually. Maintaining too formal a structure of relationships inevitably inhibits the way a system works" (Dunbar 1996:206).

The department meeting itself can be an opportunity for interaction. You, as Chair, can help increase members' interaction as you name the members of committees, selecting some members from among those who are more integrated into the group and some who are less integrated. Another helpful way of developing a sense of 'groupness' among department members is to ensure that their faculty offices are physically proximate so that they inadvertently 'run into' each other and have an opportunity to socialize during the day. Having offices separated down a long corridor, or even worse, locating them on different building floors, almost wholly inhibits interaction.

Group integration can be increased by structuring official opportunities for interaction and by encouraging informal interaction – "sociality for its own sake - to make individuals consciously aware of their membership of the workforce as a social entity." The value of belonging to the department can be reinforced not "through good management and consultation, but by invoking the natural capacity of a well-organized group to maintain cohesion based on mutual friendship" (Chance 1988:30). Take the department (with staff) to a local ski slope or a beach. Charter a fishing boat. Watch a ball game together. Have a movie night. Groups can confer benefits on individuals, but not without social cohesion.

Even after giving structural attention to proximity to other members, and increasing social interaction, you cannot reproduce the intimate associations that characterized bands of our Stone-Age ancestors. Remember that everyone in the Gardens was acquainted with everyone else from birth. They knew what everyone else was doing and had done throughout their lives and could predict their future behavior. This deep knowledge, their shared genes and memes, and constant gossiping (grooming at a distance) permitted them to maintain their bands even when they numbered up to 150 people.

You cannot replicate the conditions that made it possible for bands of associated families to form such large groups. Your colleagues today come from different cultures and backgrounds. You are likely to know them only through their present participation in the work of your discipline. Even though you can't have the same intimate knowledge of your colleagues as our ancestors did, you can increase such knowledge within your group. Initiate department parties. Invite department members to your house for drinks or dinner. Circulate announcements and congratulations for personal events like birthdays, weddings, births, professional awards, or book contracts. Engage in and encourage "the small, taken for granted, positive rituals that humans produce, such as nodding, smiling, handshaking, and so on...that support the social relationships between charismatics and dependents, and between the members more generally" (Power 1988:94). These activities can help hold the social fabric of the department together.

Relieve Stress

Departments, like human foraging groups, must adapt and respond to change. For our ancestors, the most critical changes to which they responded were the climate and the consequent availability of resources. Hearing experts' ideas made it possible for the less adept to accept a consensual decision without searching for solutions themselves. Their trust in expertise, and the strong bonds between temporary leaders and their followers, relieved stress and made modest change possible.

Academic departments today continue to face resource scarcity (and may soon have to respond to climate variability as well). Searching for additional resources can lead some departments to enact positive alterations in their programs or operations. At the same time, other departments may respond to change too slowly or not at all, leading to stasis or decline.

People in groups often don't adapt to change because change provokes distress. Contemporary humans have developed a vast repertoire of work avoidance mechanisms such as denial, blaming authority, or scapegoating to relieve stress and avoid the hard work required to confront these problems (Heifetz 1994). One purpose of leadership is to provide followers with what psychiatrists call a 'holding environment' in which stress related to change is regulated to facilitate working on adaptive problems. A holding environment is "a vessel within which people facing adaptive work can accomplish the necessary learning. The containing vessel comprises various sorts of glue: an authority structure, shared purposes, common identifications, civic associations, trustworthy institutions, and other bonds of community" (Heifetz 1994:258-9). The objective of a holding environment is not to eliminate stress but to control it so that people are not overwhelmed.

The band provided the safety and security of a holding environment for our hunter and gatherer ancestors. All its members were considered 'good,' and there was widespread sharing so that the fortunate helped provide for the less fortunate. Today, a holding environment can be provided in a department by sharing hopeful visions of the future, friendship, framing issues, establishing a decision-making process, and creating bonds of trust between leader and followers. Daniel Goleman (2006:277) invokes the same concept by mentioning that a good boss (like a good Chair) provides a "secure base' that is "[a] source of protection, energy, and comfort, allowing us to free our own energy." A feeling of security permits people to pay better attention to vital work without being distracted by anxiety or the fear of failure. Chairs can establish such trust and safety, so when they give tough feedback, the person receiving it not only stays more open but sees benefit in getting even hard-to-take information.

As Chair, you are responsible for making the department a holding environment for members who might otherwise be so distressed by either internal or external factors that they cannot effectively function. Internet sites, such as The Professor is Out, reveal some of the pressures that faculty face. You, as a tenured full professor, may be unaware of them. Some faculty burn out or resolve their stress by leaving the academy altogether. Lack of empathy from colleagues or higher-ups in the college is a significant cause.

Internally, department members can offer mutual support and friendship to each other. You can help relieve stress by intervening when group members receive incomplete or conflicting messages from other college officials. You can ensure that faculty members are treated fairly and receive all due process guarantees if they are in trouble. You can assure your colleagues that you will always have their backs.

Be Part of the Group

Being part of the group was a given among our foraging ancestors as they decided whose proposals to follow in any specific situation. Both leaders and followership were rewarded by group approval. Today, being accepted as an influential in an academic department requires that the group identify you as a colleague who understands the group and supports and protects it. Unless you are seen as a member of the group, perhaps as first among equals but nevertheless one who recognizes the group's spirit rather than demanding obedience, you will find it difficult, if not impossible, to get things done.

Your opportunity to be part of the group begins with your selection as Chair in a manner the department believes to have been appropriate. If you have been an inside appointment, your identity as 'one of us' may already have been established. If selected as an outside candidate, memes that help equate your discipline to an extended family with shared norms and values may facilitate your initial acceptance. To maintain that approval, you should regularly interact with group members, as a colleague rather than as an official, in both informal and formal settings.

Exercise your influence in unobtrusive ways. In an academic department, as in a foraging community of equals, remember that the people "will follow if (and only if) it pleases them" (Boehm 1999:109). And only a group member can know 'what pleases them.' Suggestions are more effective than commands.

Be Modest

Foragers in the Gardens of Eden found that maintaining their egalitarian way of life depended on their leaders' modesty. Shows of arrogance or attempts by leaders to increase their power or possessions were met with resistance and, if not prevented, could ultimately lead to splits within the group. Brashness, overstepping, or self-assertion was punishable by ridicule, ostracism, or worse. These groups defined a good leader as generous, a respected facilitator, keeping a low profile, seeking others' opinions, and self-effacing. Displaying these characteristics today should increase your influence with your colleagues.

Hunting ability was highly prized among foragers. But becoming too prestigious could lead to domination, so foraging groups developed mechanisms supported by leaders and followers to maintain an egalitarian relationship. A 20th Century anthropologist recorded an informant reporting a conversation between an accomplished hunter and a fellow band member. Reading the informant's statement provides insight into the ethos of leaders and followers in forager groups and suggests how a Chair today should behave.

> *Say that a man has been hunting. He must not come home and announce like a braggart, "I have killed a big one in the bush!" He must first sit down in silence until I or someone else comes up to his fire and asks, "What did you see today?" He replies quietly, "Ah, I'm no good for hunting. I saw nothing at all....maybe just a tiny one." Then I smile to myself because I now know that he has killed something big"* (Lee 1979:244-6).

You may be instrumental as a Chair in effecting significant program achievements, obtaining a new faculty line, preparing a major grant proposal, or promoting modifications to reduce faculty workload. Your influence on your department and college colleagues may increase by acting modestly and self-effacingly. "Exchange arrows" by giving credit to your colleagues who helped instead of boasting about your accomplishments. Adopt the hunter's modesty of 20,000 years ago. Even if you don't brag, department members will know what you did and tell others with a smile that "you got something big."

Another reason for modesty is that while leadership is essential to human existence, that does not necessarily mean that specific leaders are critical as individuals, even though most of us might like to believe otherwise. Consider, for example, Ozymandias, the great Egyptian leader millennia ago who reminded us that he was a mighty leader, the "king of kings." The inscription on the pedestal of his shattered colossal stone statue in the desert advised other leaders to "look on my works, ye Mighty, and despair." But his name, forgotten except by students who have read the poem by Shelley, reminds us that, with few exceptions, leaders are ephemeral, replaceable, and likely to be forgotten.

Provide Order

Order is critical to academic departments as well as society. The solution to humans' problems "lies in the construction or discovery of order... Men need an order within which they can locate themselves, an order providing coherence, continuity and justice" (Shils 1965:203). Hierarchy and egalitarianism both have strengths and weaknesses and minimize ambivalence and tension. Both tend to be self-perpetuating since engaging in one lessens the possibility of the other. Human groups can both share power and covet it. Altruism, sharing, cooperation - treating the larger groups as if they were "family" - is as human as domination, control, and bullying because "humans are prone to dominate and prone to submit" (Boehm 2000:147).

There are two basic ways of maintaining a group's peaceful and predictable social order: genetic and memetic. The genetic route to an orderly community is through dominance, as seen among chimpanzees and, presumably, early humans. The memetic path is through egalitarianism, as seen in the Gardens of Eden. Both systems reduce conflict, conserve energy, and limit aggression. The various ways contemporary societies and organizations are based can be seen as permutations or combinations of these two.

A Chair can help develop egalitarianism and cooperation in the department by engaging in reciprocity and acts of altruism. You should ensure that department members learn about colleagues who have contributed to the public good. Knowledge of altruistic acts can motivate others to emulate them, knowing they will likely be recognized and rewarded by the group for their efforts. Indirect reciprocity is based on the experience that people cooperate more with those they have observed cooperating with others (Price 2006). Providing order in a department satisfies your colleague's need for "affection, for self-maintenance, for justice, for self-transcendence" (Shils 1965:203).

Create Memes

You, as Chair, can influence faculty to relate constructive concepts to existing memes. Examples of such memes include faculty autonomy, academic freedom, what the faculty have done in the past, the behaviors of fabled scholars, the need for student development, due process procedures, your president's recent statement defying unjust gubernatorial interference, the value of mentoring and diversity, student rights, or the history and traditions of your discipline and institution. Alternatively, you as Chair can promulgate disruptive and destructive war-like memes about ignorant administrators, the need for higher admissions standards, the importance of defying the hierarchy, administrative indifference to faculty parking, or the imminent failure if the department or college keeps moving in the same direction.

You can affect department views on whether to support the administration or fight and disrupt it. You can regularly say things like "the college administration sucks," or "neither the trustees nor the president knows what they are doing," or "the Faculty Council has just screwed up our curriculum again. I'm ready to give up." Alternatively, you can repeat things like "we have the best department in the college," or "I'd rather be at this college than anywhere else," or "let's all go to graduation this year. Our students deserve it," or 'the dean has just approved most of our changes. She is one sharp cookie, and she has made some good suggestions. At our next department meeting, we'll discuss how we can change our other proposals to get them accepted."

What you say and consistently repeat until it 'infects' your colleagues' brains can create memes. Memes can affect how department members view their careers and educational responsibilities and how they will respond to your attempts to influence them.

Tell Stories

When our ancestors sat around the council fire to discuss life and death matters, they could not rely on statistics and analytical analyses. Instead, they told stories about what happened the last time they tried to find water, how a trading agreement with a neighboring band was ultimately negotiated, or the problems they encountered and overcame in killing a mammoth.

Leaders tell stories in an attempt to influence the perceptions of their followers. An objective analyst may attempt to fully describe a situation, provide available facts and alternative theories to help people understand it, and suggest courses of action that lead to preferred outcomes. Objective analysis is essential in aiding understanding today but may have little effect on motivating followers to action. If you are interested in moving your followers in particular directions, it would be best if you spent your time telling stories. "The artful creation and articulation of stories," says Gardner (1995:43), "constitutes a fundamental part of the leader's vocation."

A story provides a compelling narrative and interpretation of a situation. Instead of relying on dry data and accepted conventions, a story vividly explains why something has gone wrong (or right) and suggests how corrections may be made. Stories can remind department members of previous triumphs and failures. Stories should be narratives of identity, helping department members understand where they came from, their purpose, why the department is essential, and what the future looks like. Stories tell what should be feared, struggled against, or dreamed about. Stories should incorporate the "group history, founding visions, core group values, group structure and member's hopes for their future" (Frey & Sunwolf 2005:218). Stories provide a foundation for creating memes.

To be believed, your stories have to compete with many other narratives and memes that department members have heard in the past. You cannot dispel a previous narrative by arguing factually against it (whether the story is true is irrelevant), but only by telling a new narrative that is easy to understand, has potential as a meme, and is a better story. And while you can tell a story as a narrative, you can also tell a story through your behavior; both must match to be effective.

Telling stories is an indirect way of teaching. It can be a substitute for 'lecturing' or moralizing and is less likely to provoke adverse reactions. "When told in a group setting, stories help members to achieve symbolic convergence by communicating group norms and values, as well as by coordinating activity towards common goals; they are particularly effective for assimilating new members into a group culture, and for creating connections among group members." (Frey & Sunwolf (2005:2010-11)

All this assumes that you have been selected through procedures your followers believe to be proper, have the characteristics they are searching for, and view you as a leader. If these things are not true, your stories and memes will fall on fallow ground.

Listen Carefully at the Water-Cooler

Humans are hard-wired for surveillance of our environment to uncover threats and opportunities. This need for up-to-date information makes us hungry for news, particularly information involving misfortune, disaster, or deviance (Shoemaker 1996:33). These behaviors have genetic roots. Anything judged to be 'different,' whether from gossip, hearsay, or speculation, is potentially of survival interest. The meaning of 'survival' may differ for a Chair and a member of a Stone-Age band because of differences in their memes and culture, but both are consequential.

The metaphorical water cooler may be a more valuable source of information for you as a Chair than the college's sophisticated management information system. Our ancestors watched out for snakes and cave bears. Those who were most successful passed on these surveillance genes to their children, while those that were unsuccessful … well, you know what happened to them.

But while the surveillance function - the ability to spot potentially significant non-routine changes in daily life - may be facilitated by genes, what is considered a threat is a mental construct related to the memes of thoughts and ideas. Someone may have influenced others long ago because they were the first to identify an environmental threat; the same genetic impulse remains today, but the focus of attention has changed. Instead of expertise in interpreting the soft growl outside the cave, your expertise as Chair may give you the ability to sense if your faculty think layoffs are coming, a salary increase is rumored, some of your followers are discontent, or folks are angry with the dean. Sensing danger may help you work with colleagues to plan for alternative futures. Hard data are helpful under some circumstances, but to be an effective Chair you will likely spend more time schmoozing than analyzing spreadsheets.

Focus Attention

Like Stone Age bands, departments are composed of individuals with divergent and shared interests and differing levels of expertise. Group members pay attention to different things, which is why attending to diversity in a group can provide a greater understanding of potential threats or rewards in the environment. But after problems are identified, departments need some process that provides a common focus of attention if they are to function collectively. People exert influence as they become the focus of others' attention, attention is a scarce resource

(March 1982), and the process of directing attention is part of leadership.

You can influence which part of the department's environment is noticed and attended to and which of the myriad problems a department faces are to be considered. By preparing an agenda for a department meeting, you are deciding which of a potentially infinite number of issues should be the focus of the group's attention. As Chair, you determine procedures for conducting a discussion and determine who speaks, when, and control interruptions. "As anyone who has sat in committee meetings knows only too well, the [Chair's] control of the meeting is fundamental" (Dunbar 1996:196). That is why, in earlier chapters of this book, so much attention was given to the conduct of meetings.

Maintain Group Norms

Humans in foraging groups exercised social control through norms. Norms develop as the group's conformity to certain behaviors is rewarded or punished. Rewards can take the form of "acceptance and approval, signaled through seeking out respect, deference, friendship, affectionate behavior, and the like" (Power 1991:182). Punishments among human foragers could include loss of respect, avoidance, ridicule, and, in extreme cases, death.

The development of norms affects behavior without inducing the alienation created by the direct use of power. Norms can decrease the importance of leadership because of follower experience or system structures. Social norms are maintained through moral standards of reciprocity and cooperation that are genetically based and memetically enacted.

One way you can help maintain social norms is by ensuring the rewarding or punishing of those who violate the moral (or legal) code through which the elements of indirect reciprocity are maintained. Rewards are easy; punishments are tough. Chairs who punish non-reciprocators are not anti-social. On the contrary, even in the Gardens of Eden, punishers were likely to be "prosocial leaders who pay the costs of persuading and cajoling to induce cooperation from others" (Richerson & Boyd 1998:76). Even in a cooperative department, some individuals may try to satisfy their interests and challenge the group's interests. This is why the 'liberty' of individuals and subgroups must be limited and "why 'inequalities' must continuously be curbed" (Alexander 1987:187).

Establish Your Department as a Vigilant Moral Community

One prominent role of a Chair today is to shape a moral capacity in your department that balances freedom with security while encouraging the active participation required so that moral behavior is noted and reinforced. Leaders 20,000 years ago faced these same issues.

Morality. The source of our morality is as much biological as it is cultural. Morality evolves in humans in all cultures to "distinguish right from wrong, have a sense of fairness, help one another, impose rights and obligations, believe that wrongs should be redressed, and proscribe rape, murder, and some kinds of violence" (Pinker 2002:188). Persons of high moral development are guided by "near-universal ethical principles of justice, such as equality of human rights and respect for individual dignity" (Burns 1978:42). Genes have given humans the capacity for morality. Still, the specifics of what is moral in any particular community come from embedded memes.

Our genes give us an innate "tribal instinct" (Richerson and Boyd 2001:205). Our genetic heritage compels us to behave morally towards 'us' but not necessarily 'them.' Memes tell us how 'us' and 'them' can be identified and differentiated. Our genes require us to maintain social relations within our group; our memes clarify acceptable behaviors under specified conditions and how a group can properly correct and ultimately sanction group members whose behavior is not permitted. With the proper experiences, most people can move past their biological tendency towards selfishness. They can learn memes that help them control their actions. Our genes have designed us to "hate our enemies, ignore the needs of people we barely know, and distrust anybody who doesn't look like us" (de Waal 2005:235). But our memes permit us to increasingly enlarge the circle of those to whom we believe we have responsibilities (Singer 1981).

As Chair, you are responsible for enlarging the department's moral community. Our ancestors gave everyone a chance to speak as they sat around the council fire to express alternative views, and Chairs today should do the same. We know that women and members of minority groups often have opinions that differ in some respects from those of white males. Enlarging the circle in higher education to create a moral community requires that women and minority groups are included and fully participate in your department. Their presence provides different viewpoints on endemic problems in higher education, your discipline, and your department. Communicating differing opinions in department meetings can make members aware of unseen environmental threats and opportunities. It identifies a broader range of potential issues and a more expansive repertoire of possible solutions for a department to consider. As Chair, you can uniquely influence faculty selection processes that affect diversity and ensure that all members can fully participate in departmental affairs, thus creating a more moral department.

You must help maintain a balance of appropriate freedoms and equalities possible under the circumstances and remind department members of benefits received. You should initiate compromises and identify and initiate sanctions against free riders or social loafers. If a social system is based on reciprocity, the support of public goods can collapse if those who are able but don't contribute are permitted to continue to benefit.

Naturally, you always want to act morally. But how can you monitor the quality of your decisions to determine if they are moral or merely a self-justification for your interests? One way is to act or behave in the spirit of

Rawls' (1971) theory of justice, or fairness. Contemplate what you might choose to do in a specific situation and ask yourself whether you would be happy with that decision if you knew that you could instantly be transformed into any other department member subject to it. If the answer is 'no,' then the decision is amoral. Don't do it!

Vigilance. Assuming that your department acts morally, is it also vigilant? Vigilant moral communities, both 20,000 years ago and today, "make decisions about how they should live, and the effects on human life are pervasive because moral communities see and track everyone's behavior...Morality makes radically egalitarian outcomes possible for humans because morality involves a permanent coalition of an entire watchful community" (Boehm 1997:361).

Vigilance means that you and your department members are constantly alert for potential violations of the moral code to which you have subscribed. Vigilant department members should resist any internal or external attempt to give you authoritarian power, and they should hold you accountable. In the same way, you should oppose any attempt by others to increase the autocratic power of Chairs. Your department members know they have accorded you certain privileges and are alert to the requirements of a 'fair exchange.' They should agree that the rewards and authority provided by these privileges are commensurate with your benefits. If this principle of fairness is violated, your followers may withdraw their support, and your attempts at leadership will fail.

One significant conduit of information in a vigilant community is gossip, which you will remember is a form of grooming at a distance. As in the Stone Age, "gossiping provides an information network that enables an entire group to respond to transgressions on a well-informed and collective basis" (Boehm 1999:187). Gossip is one way that individuals in a department may remain vigilant. But other, more formal methods exist as well.

Like physicians or police officers, academics are often reluctant to criticize their own. After receiving tenure, non-performing department members known to their colleagues are usually not confronted, believing that "nothing can be done." But as Chair, you know that department members who do not do their share or perform at an acceptable level with impunity breed cynicism and challenge the social order. If (but only if) other department members are aware of and concerned about the 'free rider' and subscribe to a shared moral code, you can act. Discussing the Faculty Work Activity Dashboard with the free-rider may help. Having the free-rider meet with a group of productive faculty for 'fraternal correction' might be effective. Assisting with personal or professional problems or providing an opportunity to move to part-time duties or early or phased retirement may be in order.

As a final step, removal from tenure may be attempted. Tenure is sacrosanct in higher education and is appropriately safeguarded by layers of institutional bylaws and other legal protections. As our ancestors discovered, removing a particularly troublesome deviant from the band, although difficult, was sometimes necessary to maintain the group's cohesion. Removing a tenured faculty is equally difficult since it is a professional 'death sentence.' It is the most difficult decision a Chair can make, but with support from your colleagues and your college counsel, it is not impossible. If it is done, it demonstrates to the academic world that by following proper procedures, serious transgressions of accepted academic values can be punished. The institution may benefit by providing public evidence that colleges can solve their problems through self-government and do not require external interventions.

Establishing and maintaining a structure and processes that support individual freedom and the group's ability to compel conformity requires understanding and balancing the genetic and memetic forces influencing human beings. To influence without coercion is difficult. The vigilant moral community's egalitarian ethic has been expressed in coarser terms with the classic advice attributed to President Lyndon Baines Johnson: "Don't piss in the soup; everyone has to drink from the same bowl."

Try Transformation, if You Dare

Solving problems around the Stone Age council fire was a matter of survival. The group relied on past and proven ideas, myths that had stood the test of time, memories of elders, and the experiences of those who had been successful. New and untested ideas about where to find water or what to do if they encountered a stranger were unlikely to gain the group's support. Leadership that tried to transform the old ways was not welcome, and change was slow and incremental.

Change today is just as tricky, and the more comprehensive the change, the more challenging its acceptance. The higher education literature demonstrates that while transformational leadership is often advocated, attempts are rare and often fail for various reasons: Department members may benefit from the present situation and see no reason for the change; budget resources may not be forthcoming; the culture and processes of the college bureaucracy may not support it; stress in the department may make it impossible to consider new ideas. Change is hard. Even among businesses with hierarchical structures, seventy-five percent of organizational change initiatives fail (Dallas 2015). The failure rate might be even higher for tradition-bound colleges. Nevertheless, your experiences, your reading of your institution, and your belief that you have the necessary charisma may make you sense that 'now is the time.' If so, go for it, but be forewarned.

Transactional and transformational leadership are related to what has been called the constrained vision and the unconstrained vision of organized life (Pinker 2002:287-293). The constrained vision believes that we have limited knowledge, bounded rationality, and limitations to our virtue, and both leaders and followers recognize this by accepting the shortcomings of human nature. If improvements are to be made, they should be based on what is and should be satisfied with small increments. The current system is not perfect, but we know from experience that it works. These ideas, and the memes they invoke, suggest that transactional, short-term change is best.

On the other hand, the unconstrained vision suggests that we can overcome our limitations to make a better world. The institutions that seem essential to us change over time and have no inherent value. We can replace them with new structures that articulate social goals and plan bold policies to achieve them. Moreover, the existence of suffering and injustice presents us with an undeniable moral imperative. "We don't know what we can achieve until we try, and … resigning ourself to these evils as the way of the world, is unconscionable" (Pinker 2002:289). The notions that we can change, and the memes they invoke, indicate that working towards a transformational change of institutional structures and goals is best.

There are two paths, albeit narrow ones, to make departmental transformation possible through leadership without coercion. First, if followers see you as a leader with exceptional transactional achievements, the group's acceptance might be extended for transformational purposes. By first demonstrating competence and support of group norms, you may earn "idiosyncrasy credits" (Hollander 2004). These credits increase perceptions of your expertise and may permit you to engage in innovative actions. Once leadership trust and loyalty have been demonstrated, followers are sometimes willing to support change and revolutionary acts that would never be tolerated from a leader who had not earned that trust.

The second is to "create a shared perception by group members for change" (Tubbs 1978:26). If group members realize that change is necessary, the pressure for transformation can come from the group itself. Your role would be to help create structures and processes to implement the desire for change. Group resistance should be minimal. However, do not forget that even if your department favors transformational change, organizational forces outside the department may not accept it.

At all times, bear in mind the words of Machiavelli (1977, Ch. 6):

> There is nothing more difficult to take in hand, more perilous to conduct, or more uncertain in its success, than to take the lead in the introduction of a new order of things. Because the innovator has for enemies all those who have done well under the old conditions, and lukewarm defenders in those who may do well under the new. This coolness arises partly from fear of the opponents, who have the laws on their side, and partly from the incredulity of men, who do not readily believe in new things until they have had a long experience of them.

The Goal of the Chair

The Chair's goal should be progress achieved through academic and moral means. Based on genes and memes, the ideas proposed in this chapter are simple to prescribe but challenging to internalize and implement. They may provide food for thought, particularly if you are an experienced Chair searching for new concepts that might increase your department's effectiveness.

Prescriptions and proscriptions, mine and others, have a significant weakness: No one can follow or implement them all the time in real life. Acting according to one principle may contradict another. Managers and leaders are human and subject to the weaknesses that all humans are heir to, and what happens in real life often makes a mockery of our intentions. As they say, when humans plan, the gods laugh. Differences between what we say and what we do may appear hypocritical. But frequently, they merely demonstrate that you often may need to adjust your cherished goals to the changing needs of reality. Sometimes the best that can be done under present circumstances is all that can be done.

I end this book with four related admonitions. First, do not let your influence diminish over time. Managers and leaders in all organizations either know or unhappily learn that while gaining influence is one thing, retaining it over time is quite another. College presidents lose faculty support because their initial enthusiasm ultimately wanes. They become increasingly confident in their judgments, and their communications with faculty diminish. They become less open, reduce their campus visibility, become more indifferent to faculty concerns, and become increasingly authoritarian (Birnbaum 1992). I believe department Chairs may lose support for the same reasons.

To maintain support, you should continue behaving over time as you did when you were appointed. Remain enthusiastic, maintain communications with your department colleagues, and continually search for – and remain open to - new ideas. If you are to maintain influence, you must be seen as able to deal with problems for which you are responsible and for which there is no 'official solution.' You may have to re-envision issues in alternative ways and, together with your departmental colleagues, craft new ideas and behavioral repertoires.

Second, remain aware of the apish "indelible stamp of his lowly origin" of which Darwin spoke. When things aren't going the right way, it is easy to fall into the trap of becoming a despot like the alpha chimp. Human frailty can destroy a democratic system. Find a trusted colleague willing to tell truth to power and consciously fight this impulse towards authoritarianism.

Third, if you take the job, do the job. Show up. Be reliable. You are part of a large and intricate system, and other people in the college are counting on what you do to enable them to do their jobs. Some of your responsibilities may seem mundane, repetitive, boring, frustrating, incomprehensible, contradictory, inconsistent, or impossible. You may be tempted to take shortcuts, fudge data, or be less thorough than you should be. But the product of even your most innocuous management activity may be of value to someone else. The rule still applies: if you take the job, do the job. If you don't like the job, quit. Despite its challenges, others are almost always ready to take your place.

Fourth, and most importantly, to be an exemplary Chair, you must also be a good person, a moral person, a good listener, and a good department and college citizen.

After first studying small groups and then looking at the leadership practice of 20,000 years ago, you may be surprised, as I was, to discover that they end up in a similar place. Scholars of organizations call this equifinality, meaning that there are many paths to the same goals even when starting from different initial conditions. I hope that thinking about some of the ideas offered in this book helps you on the path toward influence, not because they represent unalterable truths, but because they might suggest new possibilities and help you prevent avoidable mistakes. I hope they make you more complicated and enable you to see alternative ways of enacting your role. I hope they expand your behavioral repertoire and permit you more accurately to judge which behaviors might be successful, given existing circumstances. And I hope these ideas make you feel more comfortable using your informed judgment when faced with new and unanticipated problems. Complicated yet comfortable – not a bad way of thinking about what it means to be a department Chair.

References

Alexander, R. D. (1987). *The biology of moral systems.* Aldine de Gruyter.

Ashby, E. (1962). The administrator: Bottleneck or pump? *Daedalus, Spring.* (pp. 264-278).

Axelrod, R. (1984). *The evolution of cooperation.* Basic Books.

Bailey, S. K. (1976). *The purposes of education.* Phi Delta Kappa Educational Foundation.

Balkin, J. M. (1998). *Cultural software: A theory of ideology.* Yale University Press.

Birnbaum, R. (1971). Presidential succession: An inter-institutional analysis. *Educational Record 52, (pp.133-145).*

Birnbaum, R. (1992). *How Academic Leadership Works: Understanding Success and Failure in the College Presidency.* Jossey-Bass.

Blackmore, S. (1999). *The meme machine.* Oxford University Press.

Boehm, C. (1993). *Egalitarian society and reverse dominance hierarchy. Current Anthropology, 34*(3), 227-254.

Boehm, C. (1997). Egalitarian behavior and the evolution of political intelligence. In A. Whiten & R. W. Byrne (Eds.), *Machiavellian intelligence II* (pp. 341-64). Cambridge University Press.

Boehm, C. (1999). *The natural selection of altruistic traits. Human Nature 10,* 205-252.

Boehm, C. (2000). *Hierarchy in the forest: The evolution of egalitarian behavior.* Harvard University Press.

Boyd, R. & Silk, J. B. (2003). *How humans evolved (3d edition).* Norton.

Brown, D. E. (1991). *Human universals.* McGraw-Hill.

Brown, D. J., Scott, K. A., & Lewis, H. (2004). Information processing and leadership: A review and implications for practice. In J. Antonakis, R. J. Sternberg, & A.T. Cianciolo (Eds.), *The nature of leadership* (pp. 125-147). Sage.

Buller, J. L. (2012. *The essential department chair.* Anker Publishing.

Burns, G. M. (1978). *Leadership.* Harper and Row.

Caporael, L., Wilson, D. S., Hemelrijk, C., & Sheldon, K. M. (2005). Small groups from an evolutionary perspective. In M. S. Poole & A. B. Hollingshead (eds), *Theories of Small Groups: Interdisciplinary Perspectives* pp. (369-396).

Cashdan, E. (1989). Hunters and gatherers: Economic behavior in bands. In S. Plattner (Ed.), *Economic Anthropology* (pp. 21-48). Stanford University Press.

Chance, M. R. A. (1988). *Social fabrics of the mind.* Lawrence Erlbaum Associates.

Chance, M. R. A. (1976). Attention structure as the basis of primate rank orders. In M. R. A. Chance & R. R. Larson (Eds.) *The social structure of attention (pp. 11-28),* Wiley.

Chance, M. R. A. & Jolly (1970). *Social groups of monkeys, apes, and men.* Jonathan Cape.

Chemers, M. M. (2002. Efficacy and effectiveness: Integrating models of leadership and intelligence. In R. E. Riggio, S. E. Murphy, & F. J. Pirozzolo (Eds.), *Multiple intelligences and leadership (*pp. 139-160). Lawrence Erlbaum.

Chu, D. (2021). *The department chair field manual: A primer for academic leadership.* Independently published.

Chu, D. & Veregge, S. (undated). The California State University department chair survey report. California State University Office of the Chancellor and the Academic Senate California State University.

Coats, J. (2019). F*** leadership: How to motivate and mentor your team to true success. Independently published.

Council of Independent Colleges (2016). Spring survey of department and division chairs shows diversity in appointment and compensation practices.

Dallas, H. J. (2015, October 22). 4 must-have skills for leaders to manage change. *Fortune [online]*. Available from <http://fortune.com/2015/10/22/change-leaders-managers/ >[22 March 2017]

Darwin, C. R. (1871). *The descent of man and selection in relation to sex, volume 2.* John Murray.

Dawkins, R. (2004). *The ancestor's tale: A pilgrimage to the dawn of evolution.* Houghton Mifflin.

de Waal, F. B. (1982). *Chimpanzee politics: Power and sex among apes.* Harper and Row.

de Waal, F. B. (1996). *Good natured: The origin of right and wrong in humans and other animals.* Harvard University Press.

de Waal, F. (2005). *Our inner ape.* Riverhead.

Diamond, J. M. (1992). *The third chimpanzee: The evolution and future of the human animal.* New York: HarperCollins.

Dunbar, R. I. M. (1996). *Grooming, gossip and the evolution of language.* London: Faber and Faber.

Dunbar, R. I. M. (1999). Culture, honesty and the freerider problem. In R. I. M. Dunbar, C. Knight, C., & C. Power, *The evolution of culture: An interdisciplinary view (pp. 194-213).* Rutgers University Press.

Dunbar, R. I. M. (2001). Brains on two legs: Group size and the evolution of intelligence. In F. B. M. de Waal (Ed.), *Tree of origin: What primate behavior can tell us about human social evolution* (pp. 175-191). Harvard University Press.

Durham, W. H. (1991). *Coevolution: Genes, culture and human diversity.* Stanford University Press.

Erdal, D., & Whiten, A. (1994, April). On human egalitarianism: An evolutionary product of Machiavellian status escalation? *Current Anthropology, 35*(2), 175-184.

Erdal, D., & Whiten, A. (1996). Egalitarian and Machiavellian intelligence in human evolution. In P. Mellars & K. Gibson (Eds.), *Modelling the early human mind* (pp. 139-150). MacDonald Institute for Archeological Research.

Etzioni, A. (1961). *A comparative analysis of complex organizations*. Free Press of Glencoe.

Fehr, E. & Gachter, S. (2000). Fairness and retaliation: The economics of reciprocity. *Journal of Economic Perspectives 14 (3)*, 159-181.

Fiske, A. P. (1992). The four elementary forms of sociality: Framework for a unified theory of social relations. *Psychological Review 99*, 689-723.

Flarherty, C. (2016). Forgotten chairs. Retrieved from https://www.insidehighereducation.com/news/2016/ 12/01/new-study-suggests-training-department-chairs-woefully-inadequate-most-institutions.

Freeman Jr., S., Karkouti, I. M. & Ward, K. (2020). Thriving in the midst of liminality: Perspectives from department chairs in the USA. *Higher Education 80*, 895-911.

French, R. P. J. & Raven, B. (1959). The bases of social power. In D. Cartwright (Ed.), *Studies in social power* (pp. 150-167). University of Michigan Press.

Frey, L. & Sunwolf (2005). The symbolic-interpretive perspective of group life. In M. S. Poole & A. B. Hollingshead (eds), *Theories of small groups: Interdisciplinary perspectives* (pp. 185-239).

Gardner, H. (1995). *Leading minds: An anatomy of leadership*. Basic Books.

Gibb, C. A. (1969). The principles and traits of leadership. In C. A. Gibb (Ed.), *Leadership: Selected readings* (pp. 205-222). Penguin.

Gigliotti, R.A. (2021, March). The impact of COVID-19 on academic department chairs: Heightened complexity, accentuated liminality, and competing perceptions of reinvention. *Innov High Ed., 1-18.*

Gladwell, M. (2005). *Blink: The power of thinking without thinking.* Little, Brown.

Gmelch, W. H. & Miskin, V. D. (1995). *Chairing an academic department.* Atwood Publishing.

*Goleman, D. (2006). Social intelligence: The new science of human relationships.*Bantam Books.

Greenleaf, R. K. (1977). *Servant leadership.* Paulist Press.

Hare, A. P. (1962). *Handbook of small group research.* Free Press of Glencoe.

Heifetz, R. A. (1994). *Leadership without easy answers.* Harvard University Press.

Hollander, E. P. (1969). Emergent leadership and social influence. In C. A. Gibb (Ed.), *Leadership: Selected readings* (pp. 293-306). Penguin.

Hollander, E. P. (1978). *Leadership dynamics: A practical guide to effective relationships.* The Free Press.

Hollander, E. P. (1985). Leadership and power. In G. Lindzey & E. Aronson (Eds.). *The handbook of social psychology* (pp. 485-537). Random House.

Hollander, E. P. (2004). Idiosyncrasy credit. *In The Encyclopedia of Leadership* (pp. 695-700). SAGE.

Hollander, E. P. (2006). Influence processes in leadership-followership: Inclusion and the Idiosyncrasy Credit model. In D. A. Hantula (Ed.), *Theoretical and methodological advances in social and organizational psychology* (pp. 293-700). Erlbaum.

Hollingshead, A. B., Wittenbaum, G. W., Paulus, P. B., Hurakawa, R. Y., Ancona, D. G., Peterson, R. S., Jehn, K. A., & Yoon, K. (2005). A look at groups from the functional perspective. In M. S. Poole & A. B. Hollingshead (eds), *Theories of Small Groups: Interdisciplinary Perspectives* pp. (21-61).

Hutchins, R. M. (1946). The administrator. *Journal of Higher Education 17(8),* (pp 395-407).

Jolly, A. (1999). *Lucy's legacy: Sex and intelligence in human evolution.* Harvard University Press.

Kandel, E. R. (2006). *In search of memory: The emergence of a new science of the mind.* W. W. Norton.

Knauft, B. B. (1991, August-October). Violence and sociality in human evolution. *Current Anthropology, 32*(4), 391-428.

Kouzes, J. M. & Posner. B. Z. (2003). *The leadership challenge: How to keep getting extraordinary things done in organizations.* Jossey-Bass.

Larson, R. R. (1976). Charisma: A reinterpretation. In M. R. A. Chance & R. R. Larsen (Eds.), *The social structure of attention* (pp. 253-272). Wiley.

Lawick-Goodall, J. V. (1971). *In the shadow of man.* Houghton Mifflin.

Lee, R. B. (1979). *The!Kung San: Men, women, and work in a foraging society.* Cambridge University Press.

Lind, E. A. & Tyler, T. R. (1988). *The social psychology of procedural justice.* Plenum.

Machiavelli, N. (1977). *The Prince* (R. M. Adams, Ed. & Trans). W. W. Norton.

March, J. G. (1982). Emerging developments in the study of organizations. *Review of Higher Education 6,* 1-18.

March, J. G. (1982). Emerging developments in the study of organizations. *Review of Higher Education 6,* 1-18.

March, J. G. (1984). How we talk and how we act: Administrative theory and administrative life. *In Sergiovanni, T. J. & Corbally, J. E. (1984.) Leadership and organizational culture: Perspectives on administrative theory and practice. pp.18-35.*

Masefield, J. (1946). The university. *Johns Hopkins Magazine, February,* (pp.21-30).

Mintzberg, H. (1973). *The nature of managerial work.* Harper and Row.

Mithen, S. (1990). *Thoughtful foragers: A study of prehistoric decision making.* Cambridge University Press.

Mithen, S. (1996). *The prehistory of the mind: The cognitive origins of art, religion and science.* Thames and Hudson.

Nesbitt, R. & Perrin, R. G. (1977). *The social bond.* Knopf.

Nicholson, N. (2000). *Executive Instinct: Managing the human animal in the information age.* Crown Business.

O' Meara, K., Beise, E., Culpepper, D., Musra, J. & Jaeger, A. (2020). Faculty work activity dashboards: A strategy to increase transparency. *Change 52 (3),* 34-42.

Ostrom, E. (2000, Summer). Collective action and the evolution of social norms. *The Journal of Economic Perspectives, 14*(3), 137-158.

Pinker, S. (2002). *The blank slate: The modern denial of human nature.* Viking Penguin.

Power, M. (1988). The cohesive foragers: Human and chimpanzee. In M. R. A. Chance (Ed.), *Social fabrics of the mind* (pp. 75-103). Lawrence Erlbaum Associates.

Power, M. (1991). *The egalitarians - Human and chimpanzee: An anthropological view of social organization.* Cambridge University Press.

Power, M. D. (1995, November-December). Back to the future: A commentary on "The quest for empowering organizations." *Organization Science, 6*(6), 671-679.

Price, M. E. (2006). Monitoring, reputation, and 'greenbeard' reciprocity in a Shuar work team. *Journal of Organization and Behavior, 27,* 201-219.

Rawls, J. (1971). *A theory of justice.* Harvard University Press.

Richerson, P. & Boyd, R. (1998). The evolution of human ultra-sociality. In I. *Eible-Eibesfeldt & F. Salter (Eds.) Indoctrinability, warfare and ideology: Evolutionary perspectives.* Berghan.

Richerson, P. J., & Boyd, R. (2001). The evolution of subjective commitment to groups: A tribal instincts hypothesis. In R. M. Nesse (Ed.), *Evolution and the capacity for commitment* (pp. 186-220). Russel Sage Foundation.

Richerson, P. J., & Boyd, R. (2004). *Not by genes alone: How culture transformed human evolution.* University of Chicago Press.

Savage-Rumbaugh, S. & McDonald, K. (1988). Deception and social manipulation in symbol-using apes. In R. W. Byrne & A. Whiten (Eds.), *Machiavellian intelligence: Social expertise and the evolution of intellect in monkeys, apes, and humans* (pp. 224-237). Clarendon Press.

Schneider, H. (1979). *Livestock and equality in East Africa: The economic basis for social structure.* Indiana University Press.

Service, E. R. (1971). *Primitive social organizations: An evolutionary perspective, second edition.* Random House.

Shepard, P. & Shepard, F. R. (1998). *Coming home to the pleistocene.* Shearwater Books.

Shermer, M. (2004). *The science of good and evil: Why people cheat, gossip, care, share, and follow the Golden Rule.* Times Books.

Shils, E. (1965). Charisma, order and status. *American Sociological Review, 30,* 199-213.

Shoemaker, P. J. (1996). Hardwired for news: Using biological and cultural evolution to explain the surveillance function. *Journal of Communication, 46 (3), 32-47.*

Simon, H. A. (1947). *Administrative behavior: A study of decision-making processes in administrative organizations.* Macmillan.

Singer, P. (1981). *The expanding circle.* Farrar, Straus and Giroux..

Slosson, E. E. (1910). *Great American universities.* Macmillan.

Tooby, J. & Cosmides, L. (1992). The psychological foundations of culture. In J. H. Barkow, L. Cosmides & J. Tooby (Eds.), *The adapted mind: Evolutionary psychology and the generation of culture* (pp. 19-136). Oxford University Press.

Tubbs, S. L. (1978). *A systems approach to small group interaction, Second Edition.* Addison-Wesley.

Vonnegut, K. Jr. (1999). *Wampeters, Forma and Granfalloons.* Dial Press.

Wade, N. (2006). *Before the dawn: Recovering the lost history of our ancestors.* Penguin.

Weber, M. (1947). *The theory of social and economic organization*. The Free Press.

Weissner, P. (1996). Leveling the hunter: Constraints on the status quest in foraging societies. In P. Wiessner & W. Schiefenhovel (Eds.), *Food and the status quest: An interdisciplinary perspective* (pp. 171-91). Berghahn Press.

Wheeler, D. W., Seagren, A.T., Becker, L.W., Kinley, E. R., Mlinek, D. D. & Robson, K. J. (2008). *The academic chair's handbook,* Second Edition. Jossey-Bass.

Wickenden, D. (2022, February). Late harvest. *New Yorker.*

Wrangham, R. W. (2001). Out of the Pan, into the fire: How our ancestors' evolution depended on what they ate. In F. B. M. de Waal (Ed.), *Tree of origin: What primate behavior can tell us about human social evolution (pp. 1231-143),* Harvard University Press.

Wrangham, R. W. & Peterson, D. (1996). *Demonic males: Apes and the origins of human violence.* Houghton Mifflin.

Zahneis, M. (2022, March). The faculty job (almost) no one wants. *Chronicle of Higher Education*, pp. 18,23.

Other Books by Robert Birnbaum

Creative academic bargaining: Managing conflict in the unionized college and university (1980). Teachers College Press.

Maintaining diversity in higher education (1983). Jossey-Bass.

How colleges work: The cybernetics of academic organization and leadership (1988). Jossey-Bass.

ASHE reader in organization and governance of higher education (editor) (1983, 1984.). Ginn Press.

Cooperation in academic negotiations: A guide to mutual gains bargaining (with R, J. Begin & B. Brown) (1985). Institute for Management and Labor Relations, Rutgers University.

Faculty in governance: The role of senates and joint committees in academic decision making (editor) (1991). Jossey-Bass.

How academic leadership works: Understanding success and failure in the college presidency (1992). Jossey-Bass.

Management fads in higher education: Where they come from, what they do, why they fail (2000). Jossey-Bass.

Speaking of higher education: The academic's book of quotations (2004). American Council on Education/ Praeger.